RESIDUAL INCOME FOR MUSIC PRODUCERS

YOUR COMPLETE GUIDE ON HOW TO START EARNING MULTIPLE STREAMS OF INCOME AS A MUSIC PRODUCER

ALLEN **FAT FINGERS** BROWN

RESIDUAL INCOME FOR MUSIC PRODUCERS

**Copyright © 2024 by Build Our Kingdom Publishing, LLC
and Allen Brown
Published by Build Our Kingdom Publishing, LLC**

All rights reserved. This book or any portion thereof may not be reproduced or used in any manner whatsoever without the express written permission of the publisher except for the use of brief quotations in a book review.

Printed in the United States of America
1st Edition January 2024 First Printing

ISBN for paperback: 978-1-7350588-3-2
ISBN for eBook: 978-1-7350588-2-5

Build Our Kingdom Publishing, LLC. 560 Main St, Stroudsburg, PA 18360

Edited by: Allen Brown

Although the publisher and the author have made every effort to ensure that the information in this book was correct at press time and while this publication is designed to provide accurate information in regard to the subject matter covered, the publisher and the author assume no responsibility for errors, inaccuracies, omissions, or any other inconsistencies herein and hereby disclaim any liability to any party for any loss, damage, or disruption caused by errors or omissions, whether such errors or omissions result from negligence, accident, or any other cause.

This publication is meant as a source of valuable information for the reader, however, it is not meant as a substitute for direct expert assistance. If such a level of assistance is required, the services of a competent professional should be sought.

All producer names and likenesses used in this book are granted by the terms and conditions of BuyBeats.com Inc., which stipulate that the company may use names and likenesses in any promotional materials for BuyBeats.com. For more details, please refer to the terms and conditions available on the BuyBeats.com website at https://buybeats.com/content/terms.

Table of Contents

Letter From Founder v

Dedication vi

Introduction A Music Producer's Guide to Transitioning from Uncertainty to Certainty 1

Chapter 1 Beats, Business, and Beyond: Navigating the BuyBeats.com Universe 7

Chapter 2 Why BuyBeats.com? Playing the Long Game for Financial Success 19

Chapter 3 Your Guide to Getting Paid: Affiliate Marketing Business Model Revealed 29

Chapter 4 Setting the Stage for Your Success on BuyBeats.com 37

Chapter 5 Mastering Your Dashboard for Lasting Success 45

Chapter 6 Boost Your Residual Income Gains with the Blue Share Buttons... 59

Chapter 7 Embrace Additional Key Features Tailored for Your Success on BuyBeats.com 73

Phase 2 Growing Your Customers on BuyBeats.com 85

Chapter 8 Building Your Social Media Presence for Success ... 91

Chapter 9 A Blueprint for Genuine Connections and Endless Prosperity.. 99

Chapter 10 Learn The Art of Attracting Prospects to Grow Lasting Residual Income 107

Chapter 11 (DM) Direct Messaging Mastery - Applying Cialdini's Principles 115

Chapter 12 Lead Generation: 21 Marketing Ideas for Music Producers to Generate Leads 125

Chapter 13 Case Study: $4,000 in Residual Income Earned in 3 Months! 145

Phase 3 My Millionaire Mentor's Wisdom at 19: Personal Insights for Success 159

Chapter 15 How I Turned $8 into Millions 165

Chapter 16 Maximizing Your Assets: The Blueprint for Obtaining Wealth 171

Chapter 17 Mindset Mastery for Music Producers 181

Chapter 18 Sample Marketing Plan: A Blueprint Tailored for Music Producers 187

Chapter 19 Artificial Intelligence: AI Tools That Can Enhance Music Producers' Success 195

Chapter 20 Supercharge Your Progress: Propel Goals with 8 Step Formula! 203

Chapter 21 Music Producer Self-Assessment Worksheet 217

Closing Remarks 225

Letter From Founder

Dear fellow music producer,

This book is your complete insider guide on how to build a steady income on BuyBeats.com. It's disheartening to see some music producers only skimming the surface, while others start making money right away. In today's world, it has to be about more than just selling your beats; it's about securing streams of income that echo long after the initial work is done – the kind of income that awaits future producers like you!

Take your time to absorb every word in these pages, for within them lies the key to transforming your production journey. I assure you, investing your attention will mark a pivotal moment in your music production career.

Questions or thoughts? Don't hesitate to reach out. Assistance awaits to help you cultivate a sustainable income. This book, my friend, holds the keys to your success on the BuyBeats.com platform and beyond!

Best regards,

Allen Brown A.K.A. *Fat Fingers*

Dedication

This book is dedicated to my son, Josiah, AKA Sensei Jay. Without him diving into music production, BuyBeats.com might not have come to life. I also dedicate this book to all the producers I've ever made money with and those I'm going to continue making money with.

Last but certainly not least, a special dedication to my brother, the Grammy Music Producer, Rockwilder, who embarked on the journey of rocbattle.com with me, playing a pivotal role in the millions paid to producers worldwide. You all are the reason why I grind so hard to get things done. As we journey through the beats and melodies, may this book stand as a testament to the camaraderie that defines our community. Here's to the beats, the hustle, and the unwavering dedication we share.

Introduction

A Music Producer's Guide to Transitioning from Uncertainty to Certainty

Why is it that some producers join BuyBeats.com and start making hundreds of dollars their first month and others don't. Well, we are about to jump all the way in on this topic so you don't miss out on a system and opportunity that's revolutionizing the beat selling industry.

As a producer, you can either operate in uncertainty or certainty. Many producers struggle because they don't grasp the difference, and as a result, they suffer from their own misinformation. Let me break it down in a way that brings clarity to what I'm sharing.

THE UNCERTAIN PATH: SELLING BEATS ONLINE

Some producers put their beats online for sale, relying solely on the marketing and promotion from others to get beat sales. Occasionally, they may achieve a beat sale, and selling an exclusive beat for $400 can indeed be a great accomplishment. But the question remains: when will the next $400 beat sale come? This is the realm of uncertainty, where the producer can't predict when the next sale will happen—$300, $400, or even a $1000 beat sale, when will it come again!

BUILDING WITH CERTAINTY

Building with certainty involves incorporating residual income into your system. You continue your marketing and promotion efforts while being more certain about the income that will come to you every month. With BuyBeats.com, there's no more guessing; you can be almost sure with 100% certainty about the money you'll make monthly. This is achieved by setting yourself up in a system that continually brings you residual income for the same work you would have done in the uncertain system.

THE POWER OF RESIDUAL INCOME

Life develops based on what you can see; it's all about the perspective you have. Some producers see what BuyBeats.com can do and run with it and start building their residual income right away. If they see they made $5 in the first month without selling beats, that's a reason for celebration because that $5 can turn into $15 the next month and $30 the next. The money keeps growing bigger without selling beats because of the system that's all about residual income, which you are going to learn all about in this book.

CASE STUDIES ON BUYBEATS.COM

I'll share a few case studies in this book about producers on the platform who have gone up to $300 and $400 in the first month of membership alone, steadily growing because they understand the system and what it means to build residual income as a producer.

BEING USED ON OTHER PLATFORMS

Here is the real truth. While you're marketing and promoting on other platforms, you're actually making someone else benefit from your time and effort without getting paid for it. Let's say you drive

1000 recording artists to your beats from posts you made on Instagram over time. Only to see that no one purchased your beats. That's actually a tragedy even if you send that same traffic to your own website. It's completely unfruitful for you, but not for the platform owner. For them, you are building their membership, you build their brand, and to top it off, they don't even say thank you. They clearly benefit from your promotional efforts, and you get nothing in return. That's called being used.

EARNING FOR EVERY ACTION ON BUYBEATS.COM

Now, imagine another platform that says, "You're driving all this traffic; we'll start giving you commissions for the activity that produces money from your traffic." If someone signs up to the platform because of your efforts, you will start getting paid for their activity. If they get a subscription, you get a percentage. If they purchase beats, whether yours or another producer's, you get a percentage. If someone plays your beats or beats of another music producer you referred, you get paid. These rewards are not just one-time; it's every time "your customers" conduct activity on this new platform for a lifetime. The tables have turned, and the game has changed for you.

UNDERSTANDING THE BUYBEATS.COM DIFFERENCE

I meet producers every day who say to me, "Fat Fingers, I don't know about BuyBeats.com; I haven't sold a beat for 2 months." I think to myself, "You missed the point and thought we were like other platforms where it's only about selling beats." What I feel like saying is, "Did you invite any recording artists or other music producers to the platform to become your customers so you can start growing your residual income and get paid? "or "Did you invite artists to listen to your beats so you can get paid for the streams?" or "Did you share any of your links with other producers to tell them they can get paid for beat plays as well as 12 other ways?"

These are all things producers and artists do everywhere else for free, but somehow didn't see they get paid for all those things on BuyBeats.com. But I can't force anyone to change their perspective on what they see or understand. Still, some producers see the bigger picture and start generating cash right away without selling their beats. Some do sign up, leave, and then come back, after realizing the depth of what BuyBeats.com offers. Just think, after working the system, it could generate way more than your monthly membership, regardless if selling your beats or not.

EVOLVING AS A MUSIC PRODUCER

As a music producer, I know the feeling of waiting for people to like and purchase my beats. It's not a good feeling. Back in the 90s when I started selling beats, I sold many beats for $500, but I couldn't predict when the next sales would come. This caused me to be extremely frustrated more times than I can count. Now, looking at the systems I've built online, they are all designed to help producers financially or gain exposure for their talent and grow smarter financially.

CHANGING THE GAME WITH BUYBEATS.COM

What you're about to read is the blueprint for success on the platform, changing the game to bring more certainty to your life. Hopefully, this helps you understand how you can build with more certainty, avoiding the uncertainty of not knowing when the next sale is coming in, if it comes in at all.

PAVING THE WAY FOR CERTAINTY

Now, as you delve into the pages of this book, consider it more than just techniques and secrets. It's a blueprint for success with BuyBeats.com and beyond. In a world where many producers struggle due to a lack of marketing knowledge or unfair platform practices, BuyBeats.com is changing the game.

HERE'S HOW THIS BOOK IS BROKEN DOWN FOR YOU:

Phase 1: Unveiling BuyBeats.com - Explore the foundational aspects of BuyBeats.com and learn all the ways to monetize the platform. From understanding the program's core to navigating your dashboard, it's all about laying the groundwork for your successful journey.

Phase 2: Elevating Your Reach and Earnings - Delve into the intricacies of promotion and marketing strategies that fuel your growth on BuyBeats.com. Uncover the secrets of leveraging links, campaigns, and outreach tools to amplify your presence and earnings.

Phase 3: Beyond BuyBeats.com - Navigating Success with Unconventional Wisdom This phase isn't just about BuyBeats.com; it's a compass for your journey in the world of success, guided by unconventional wisdom. Join me as I go into a realm where personal and professional insights merge.

From distinctive perspectives to proven results, each chapter unfolds like a conversation between mentors, sharing the secrets that fuel genuine growth. Step into a space where success is more than a destination—it's a philosophy, and you're invited to be part of the narrative.

As you navigate through these pages, I encourage you to adopt a mindset that sees challenges as opportunities. The goal is not just to sell beats but to build a sustainable and diverse income stream that transcends the traditional boundaries of the music production industry.

So, without further ado, let's continue this journey into the world of BuyBeats.com, where beats, business, and boundless opportunities collide.

Chapter 1

Beats, Business, and Beyond: Navigating the BuyBeats.com Universe

Welcome to the world of BuyBeats.com – a space where beats meet business, and where music producers transform into savvy marketers. Before we dive into the nitty-gritty of 'Residual Income for Music Producers: The Complete Guide on How to Unlock Multiple Streams of Income with BuyBeats.com,' let me pull back the curtain and share a bit about my journey and the essence of this book.

With over 25 years in the beat selling business, I've witnessed producers soar to success and others struggle to take off. Through these years, I've realized that it's not just about the beats you create; it's about applying the right principles and knowledge to navigate the online market successfully.

I've been fortunate to pay millions to producers online, run successful websites that generated millions, but let me be clear – I'm no different from you. I've chosen hard work, followed wealth principles, learned from the best, and strategically paved my way to success. This book is my attempt to hand over those tools, to empower you to build something you can be proud of, and to guide you toward the financial freedom you crave.

In a world where some producers see only obstacles – the rise of AI, free tools, and easy beat-making software– I choose to embrace it all. This book is a call to adopt a mindset that doesn't see challenges but opportunities. Because remember, it's not the best producers who make all the money; it's the smartest ones who follow the rules, learning how to get their material in front of the right people at the right time.

As you journey through these pages, know that I've got your best interest at heart. I'm pouring out all my knowledge and wisdom about the beat industry and online success. No secrets held back. By the time you finish this book, you'll not only have a better mindset but powerful information to reshape your approach to making money with music production.

Now, let's talk about BuyBeats.com. I created it to offer music producers the chance to build residual income and leverage their time and efforts. While there have been beat platforms before, none to date have provided scalability and financial freedom like BuyBeats.com.

THE GENESIS OF BUYBEATS.COM: A CHANCE ENCOUNTER IN 2008

Back in 2008, the story of BuyBeats.com began with an unexpected message on my AIM (AOL Instant Messenger). I was immersed in my work when a message popped up on my screen. "Hey, are you Allen Brown?" the message read. It was a typical online exchange, cautious and laced with a bit of mystery. I responded, "It depends, who's asking?"

To my surprise, the mysterious messenger revealed himself to be a fellow producer named George. His opening line wasn't just a casual greeting; it was the prelude to a journey that would shape the future of BuyBeats.com. George expressed admiration for the success of Rocbattle.com, a music production platform I owned where I hosted thousands of music producers and paid millions to producers around the world. The virtual conversation evolved, and George shared his aspirations for a collaborative effort.

"I like what you're doing with Rocbattle.com," George typed, "I like how you've grown it and the success that it has. I wanted to know if you would be interested in doing a big platform site with me."

Now, at that moment, my attention was piqued. The prospect of partnering with someone who not only acknowledged my success but also wanted to build another big platform was intriguing. So, I continued to let him share his thoughts with me. As our conversation continued, George dropped the bombshell. He disclosed to me that he was the owner of the domain name "buybeats.com."

The impact of that statement reverberated through our virtual exchange. In the world of beat production and online platforms, the value of a domain name can't be overstated. The better the domain, the more likely one is to be successful. BuyBeats.com was not just a name; it was a potential game-changer. In the realm of online beat selling, the significance of a domain name is paramount, and George had one that immediately caught my attention.

Caught in the allure of this domain, I found myself saying, "Wait, you own the domain name buybeats.com?"

George confirmed, and suddenly, the possibilities seemed limitless. In the realm of beat production, having a domain name that perfectly aligns with your business is akin to striking gold. We continued our conversation, and George proposed a 50/50 joint venture, a partnership that could revolutionize the online beat-selling landscape.

Our initial attempts to establish an advertising network for BuyBeats.com didn't pan out as we envisioned. The complexities of the online market posed challenges, and our ambitious plans hit roadblocks. Despite our best efforts, BuyBeats.com struggled to take off.

THE TURNING POINT IN 2012: OWNERSHIP AND LEGAL CHALLENGES

Fast forward to 2012, a pivotal year in the journey of BuyBeats.com. Legal complexities began to overshadow our initial ambitions. As we sought to trademark the "BuyBeats.com" name, we faced opposition from Beats Electronics, adding a layer of intricacy to our endeavors.

In the midst of these legal challenges, a unique situation unfolded. George, my partner in this venture, expressed concerns about potential repercussions from Dr. Dre, who was formerly a member of the rap group NWA. The legal battles and the opposition from a formidable entity like Beats Electronics seemed daunting to George, and he decided to step back.

In a candid exchange, George told me, "I don't really want to fight with Dr. Dre's company anymore."

"Why?" I asked.

"I don't want to mess with NWA because I don't want those guys to come to my house and do anything to me," he confessed.

I stood there, somewhat taken aback by the unexpected turn of events. In my mind, the legal battles were par for the course in business, but George had different concerns.

He continued, "Whatever you do, I want to take my name off the trademark site because these guys know my address, and I don't want any problems."

This revelation left me in a momentary state of disbelief. The idea that legal battles could escalate to the point of fearing physical repercussions was something I hadn't anticipated. Nonetheless, this turn of events led to a unique opportunity.

A few days after this conversation, George came back to me with a proposition. "Do you want to just own the buybeats.com name 100% by yourself? I want out of it."

Without hesitation, I agreed. We negotiated a settlement, and for the small sum of $1,200, I became the complete owner of BuyBeats.com. It was a swift and unexpected turn of events that altered the trajectory of BuyBeats.com's ownership and set the stage for the next chapter in its journey.

HANDOVER AND HURDLES: A SOLO JOURNEY WITH BEATS ELECTRONICS

One thing George mentioned before signing the paper to hand over the BuyBeats.com name was, "I feel like God made BuyBeats.com for you, like if I never was supposed to have it after I met you." I distinctly remember thinking, "I believe it." With George out of the picture, I found myself in a tussle with Beats Electronics.

In 2013, negotiations for the trademark were underway, and my attempts to secure a payment due to prior use faced resistance from Beats Electronics. The tug-of-war continued until a pivotal moment when Beats Electronics disclosed a game-changing detail — Apple was in the process of acquiring Beats Electronics.

This revelation set the stage for a crucial decision. Beats Electronics warned that unless I settled before Apple finalized the acquisition, I would be facing Apple's formidable legal team. The challenges and costs involved in such a legal battle with Apple became apparent, leading me to make the practical choice to settle.

The settlement terms were straightforward — I agreed not to sell headphones on BuyBeats.com. In return, the trademark was granted solely in my name. The legal tussle concluded, marking the beginning of BuyBeats.com's journey as my sole proprietorship in the ever-evolving landscape of online platforms.

THE RESURGENCE IN 2021: A BUILDING, A STUDIO, AND BUYBEATS.COM REBORN

Fast forward to 2021, and BuyBeats.com found new life in an unexpected place – an 11-unit multi-complex building. Transitioning to this era, my journey into commercial real estate not only brought about more financial investments but unexpectedly breathed new life into BuyBeats.com. As I ventured into commercial real estate, this building, consisting of two storefronts and nine apartments, became more than just an investment; it became a symbol of my commitment to residual income. Purchasing an asset that generates money every month while you sleep is a goal that everyone should aspire to. In the world of financial wisdom, the 11-unit building epitomized the power of residual income – an asset that steadily generates profits, mirroring the vision I had for BuyBeats.com.

This building was not just about real estate; it became the catalyst for the resurgence of BuyBeats.com. My son, Sensei Jay, expressed a growing interest in producing beats, and with ample space in the building's basement, he asked me if we could build a studio there. Little did we know that this decision would breathe new life into BuyBeats.com.

Once the studio was complete, my son voiced his desire to sell beats on the internet. BuyBeats.com had been sitting dormant and suddenly became the perfect domain for this endeavor. However, we decided to reinvent BuyBeats.com, not just as a beat-selling platform, but as a hub for multiple streams of income for producers. One of the key principles I wanted to instill in this new iteration of BuyBeats.com was the concept of residual income. It's the idea of building assets that continue to generate income long after the initial effort. The 11-unit building itself was a testament to this principle, and BuyBeats.com was to be the vehicle through which music producers could achieve similar financial goals.

BUYBEATS.COM EVOLVES: PIONEERING MULTIPLE INCOME STREAMS

Our vision for BuyBeats.com extended beyond the conventional beat-selling model. While we initially started by paying out referral and subscription fees, our commitment to providing multiple income streams for producers and artists continued to evolve.

BuyBeats.com became the first website to compensate producers for beat plays alone. This meant that producers earned money even if their beats weren't flying off the digital shelves. We expanded our innovative approach by rewarding artists for merely listening to beats on the platform.

The evolution didn't stop there. As I write this book, many producers on the site are cashing in from more than just beat sales, a significant feat compared to traditional beat-selling platforms. The goal is not just to replicate the success of the past but to surpass it. BuyBeats.com aims to revolutionize the way producers earn, offering them additional streams of income beyond beat sales.

BEYOND THE BEATS AND BUSINESS

Now, as you navigate through these pages, adopt a mindset that turns challenges into opportunities. Beyond the beats and business, this guide is your ally in reshaping your approach to music production and marketing. The goal isn't just selling beats; it's constructing a sustainable and diverse income stream that defies the traditional boundaries of the music production industry.

As you turn the page, get ready for insights that directly align with the challenges and pivotal moments you may encounter on your path to success. This isn't just about BuyBeats.com's journey; it's about equipping yourself with the tools and knowledge essential for your own unique journey.

The Journey of Resilience: From Beats to Business Mastery

Logical Point: The introduction encapsulates a journey of over 25 years in the beat-selling domain, emphasizing that success isn't merely about creating beats but applying principles to navigate the online market. It sets the stage for a narrative that transcends beat-making, underlining the importance of strategy and knowledge. Why limit yourself to beat creation when the journey to success involves mastering the principles of the online market?

The Essence of Strategic Success: A Beacon of Wisdom

Logical Point: The author's story, a blend of paying millions to producers, running successful websites, and strategically navigating challenges, becomes a beacon of wisdom. It's a testament that success is not exclusive but achieved through hard work, wealth principles, and learning from the best. Why fumble in the dark when this book offers a torch of knowledge to guide you toward financial freedom?

Navigating Challenges as Opportunities: A Mindset Shift

Logical Point: In a world where challenges abound – AI, free tools, and easy beat-making software – the call is to embrace them as opportunities. The narrative urges a mindset shift that doesn't perceive obstacles but sees avenues for growth. Why succumb to challenges when you can adopt a mindset that turns adversity into opportunities?

The Power of Strategic Positioning: Beats and Business Unite

Logical Point: BuyBeats.com is introduced as a platform born not just out of necessity but from strategic positioning. It symbolizes the convergence of beats and business, challenging the notion that beat-selling is confined to a linear model. Why settle for a platform that segregates beats from business when BuyBeats.com integrates them into a unified approach?

Ownership Chronicles: The Genesis and Resurgence of BuyBeats.com

Logical Point: The narrative unfolds the saga of BuyBeats.com, from a chance encounter on AIM in 2008 to legal challenges in 2012, and its solo journey against Beats Electronics. The story becomes a testament to resilience and strategic ownership. Why settle for mere beat-selling platforms when BuyBeats.com's ownership story exemplifies a journey through challenges to resurgence?

Real Estate and Residual Income: The 11-Unit Building Epitome

Logical Point: The unexpected revival of BuyBeats.com through a commercial real estate venture becomes a profound lesson in residual income. The 11-unit building symbolizes more than an investment – it becomes a representation of the power of assets that generate money consistently. Why limit your financial goals to beat sales when BuyBeats.com provides a blueprint for achieving residual income?

Evolution of Income Streams: Pioneering Beyond Beat Sales

Logical Point: BuyBeats.com's evolution, compensating producers for beat plays and rewarding artists for listening, breaks away from traditional beat-selling models. It becomes a pioneering force in offering diverse income streams. Why confine yourself to platforms that only reward beat sales when BuyBeats.com is at the forefront of reshaping how producers earn?

A Blueprint for Producer Empowerment: Success Beyond Boundaries

Logical Point: The guide is not just a collection of techniques; it's a blueprint for success with BuyBeats.com. In a world where marketing knowledge and platform practices can hinder success, BuyBeats.com emerges as a game-changer. Why struggle on platforms with limitations when BuyBeats.com offers a comprehensive guide to building a sustainable and diverse income stream?

Comparison to Ponder:

When weighing the logical points embedded in this introduction against the conventional beat-selling landscape, BuyBeats.com emerges as a platform that not only facilitates beat sales but transforms producers into strategic entrepreneurs. Why settle for platforms that focus solely on beat transactions when BuyBeats.com provides a logical and comprehensive approach to building a prosperous future?

Chapter 2

Why BuyBeats.com? Playing the Long Game for Financial Success

As the CEO of BuyBeats.com, I'm thrilled to take you on a journey that transcends the ordinary, a journey into the heart of why BuyBeats.com is not just a platform but a game-changer for music producers. This chapter explores the essence of BuyBeats.com, exploring how it redefines success, challenges old mindsets, and propels you toward a future of limitless possibilities.

THE POWER OF GETTING PAID: SIMPLIFIED

Let's start with the basics – getting paid. At BuyBeats.com, we've cracked the code to ensure that every action you take translates into real, tangible rewards. Beyond selling beats, it's about establishing a consistent income stream that flows even when you're not actively promoting beat sales.

Imagine this: every time an artist plays your beats, you get paid. Yes, you heard it right. We believe in rewarding you for your creativity, not just when a beat sells but when it's appreciated. It's a fundamental shift from the traditional model, and it's a shift that puts money in your pocket, consistently.

LEVERAGING YOUR EFFORTS FOR FUTURE GAINS

Now, let's talk about leverage. Most platforms out there focus on the here and now – you sell a beat, you get paid. But what if I told you there's a smarter way? BuyBeats.com introduces a groundbreaking concept: leverage. From day one, you're not just a producer; you're an affiliate/business partner on BuyBeats.com. Your every move, every share, becomes a potential source of income.

This isn't about working harder; it's about working smarter. When you build a network, invite fellow artists and music producers, you're not just growing the platform; you're growing your income. This approach shifts the game by making your efforts today the foundation for ongoing rewards tomorrow.

THE POWER OF PATIENCE: BREAKING FREE FROM INSTANT GRATIFICATION

The path to success in any creative field is rarely paved with instant gratification. For aspiring music producers, the initial dream of selling beats and living the rockstar life can quickly fade when faced with the reality of building a music production career. BuyBeats.com can be a powerful tool for those with the right mindset, a mindset that embraces hard work, perseverance, and a willingness to learn. Those who see the platform as a shortcut to overnight fame are likely to find themselves disillusioned and defeated. But for those who approach it with dedication and a willingness to put in the time, BuyBeats.com can be the steppingstone to a long and fulfilling income source for years.

Here's where the narrative takes a turn. BuyBeats.com isn't promising instant gratification; it's promising a sustainable, long-term success story. The decision to quit after a short stint isn't a flaw in the platform but a misalignment of expectations many producers have. It's a mindset rooted in the old paradigm of immediate rewards.

BuyBeats.com challenges this mindset by presenting a revolutionary approach. Instead of chasing quick wins, we advocate for the strategic building of assets – a network of artists and producers who contribute to your ongoing success. It's a shift from the culture of immediate results to the culture of long-term prosperity.

UNDERSTANDING YOUR ASSETS ON BUYBEATS.COM

On BuyBeats.com, the artists and music producers you invite serve as your invaluable assets, playing a pivotal role in shaping your long-term success. Through the platform's referral system, each new artist or music producer you bring in not only expands your network but also contributes to the overall growth of BuyBeats.com.

Consider this: every action taken by those you refer translates into tangible income for you. Whether they're buying your beats or engaging in other platform activities, it all adds up to financial gains for you. The more artists and producers you introduce to the platform, the greater your potential for a scalable and sustained source of income over time.

It's not just about immediate financial benefits. By strategically building a network on BuyBeats.com, you're investing in a future filled with long-term rewards. The relationships you form on the platform can evolve into ongoing collaborations, consistent beat sales, and a variety of opportunities that continue to generate income year after year.

Beyond the numbers, BuyBeats.com encourages a personal and cultural shift in your approach. Move away from the allure of quick wins and embrace a mindset that focuses on long-term prosperity. This shift not only benefits you individually but also contributes to fostering a community on the platform that thrives on sustainable growth.

In essence, the artists and music producers you invite are more than just contributors – they're your allies in the journey toward sustained prosperity on BuyBeats.com. Through the referral system, income generation, long-term collaborations, and a shared cultural shift, these individuals become your invaluable assets, consistently providing substantial rewards for your enduring success.

COMPARING PLATFORMS: A REALITY CHECK

Let's address the elephant in the room – the comparison with other beat-selling platforms. The reality is that many platforms focus on a transactional model – you sell a beat, you get paid. Although this approach may yield results for some, it falls short of embracing the principles that ensure sustained success.

BuyBeats.com stands apart by embracing the wealth principles of leverage, residual income, networking, and community building. It's not just about selling beats; it's about creating a thriving ecosystem where your every action contributes to your long-term prosperity.

A GLIMPSE INTO THE FUTURE: 5 YEARS FROM NOW

Let's fast forward five years into the future. Picture two scenarios:

Scenario 1: You stuck to the old paradigm, hopping between platforms, seeking immediate beat sales. Your income is transactional, directly tied to each beat sold. You may have made some quick wins, but the foundation for sustained success is absent.

Scenario 2: You embraced the BuyBeats.com approach. You strategically built a network of artists and music producers, diversified your income streams, and leveraged the power of residual income. Every action you took in the initial years continues to pay off, creating a robust financial ecosystem.

Which scenario aligns with your vision of success?

ALIGNING WITH YOUR VISION OF SUCCESS:

Let's take a deeper look into the short-term and long-term effects of the decisions you make when it comes to your music production career.

1. SHORT-TERM VS. LONG-TERM GOALS:

Old Way of Thinking (Scenario 1): Imagine it's like sprinting in a race, but every race is different, and you're only focused on winning each sprint. This way of thinking leads to quick wins, but it's like running without a map – you may not know where you're headed in the long run.

New Way of Thinking (Scenario 2): Now, picture it as a marathon. You're not just sprinting; you're strategically planning each step, building a route for long-term success. BuyBeats.com acts as your navigator, offering tools and a platform that aligns with this smarter, long-term mindset.

2. RISK TOLERANCE:

Old Way of Thinking (Scenario 1): It's like putting all your eggs in one basket. Depending solely on beat sales can be risky because if the market shifts or trends change, you're left with a basket full of broken eggs.

New Way of Thinking (Scenario 2): Think of it as having multiple baskets. By diversifying income streams, you're not reliant on just one source. With BuyBeats.com, you're equipped with a platform that encourages and facilitates this diversified approach, reducing risks associated with dependency on a single revenue channel.

A PLATFORM THAT GROWS WITH YOU:

Your journey as a music producer is dynamic, marked by growth and evolution. BuyBeats.com isn't a static platform; it's an evolving ecosystem that grows with you. As you refine your skills and expand your network, our platform adapts to accommodate your changing needs.

Think of BuyBeats.com as a collaborative partner in your creative journey, providing the tools and opportunities to propel you forward at every stage of your career.

DIVERSIFYING YOUR INCOME STREAMS

Let's break free from the monotony of waiting for beat sales. BuyBeats.com offers you a multitude of income streams. It goes beyond the beat-centric model, ensuring that you earn from beat plays, subscriptions, and beat sales. Our referral program empowers you to earn a recurring monthly income from the subscriptions of those you invite.

Think about it – why limit yourself to a single source of income when BuyBeats.com opens doors to a plethora of opportunities? It's about building a resilient financial ecosystem that stands the test of time.

> **Wisdom Note: Building a Resilient Financial Ecosystem**
> **Diversification Lesson:** In the realm of finance, history teaches us the importance of diversification. The Great Depression highlighted the risks of relying on a single financial

asset. Those who diversified their investments weathered the storm more effectively.

Application to BuyBeats.com: Break free from the monotony of waiting for beat sales. BuyBeats.com offers a multitude of income streams – from beat plays to subscriptions. Diversify your income streams, building a resilient financial ecosystem that stands the test of time.

THE GAME-CHANGING PARADIGM: GET PAID WHEN THEY PLAY

Traditional platforms follow a straightforward rule – you get paid when your beat sells. But BuyBeats.com is rewriting the rules. Here, you get paid when artists play your beats. It's more than the end product; it's about the journey, appreciation, and the ongoing flow of income that comes from artists engaging with your beats.

Imagine the freedom of earning, not just from sales but from every play, every interaction. It's a paradigm shift that distinguishes BuyBeats.com from the rest.

BUILDING A COMMUNITY OF ASSETS

At BuyBeats.com, we don't just see users; we see assets. Each artist and producer you invite becomes a valuable asset in your network. As they engage with the platform, playing beats, uploading content, and generating revenue, they contribute to your ongoing income stream.

It's a community-driven model where your efforts in building a network of users result in continuous rewards. Your network becomes a powerful asset, working for you, and that's the BuyBeats.com advantage.

Principles in Focus: Leveraging Your Time and Resources. Let's take a closer look at the principles that underpin the BuyBeats.com advantage.

Leverage: In traditional models, your income is directly tied to your efforts. You sell a beat, you get paid. BuyBeats.com introduces the concept of leverage to the music production community – the ability to do the work once and reap the rewards continuously. When you invite artists and producers to the platform, you're leveraging your network to generate income every time they engage.

YOUR NETWORK AS VALUABLE ASSETS

Delving into the success of historical figures, particularly Benjamin Franklin, provides us with valuable insights into the art of networking. Franklin's achievements were not merely a result of individual brilliance but were significantly influenced by his ability to build extensive networks and foster collaborations.

Diverse Connections: Benjamin Franklin interacted with individuals from various fields—scientists, writers, politicians, and more. This diversity in his connections expanded his perspectives and allowed for a rich exchange of ideas. Similarly, on BuyBeats.com, consider engaging with a diverse community of artists and producers. Embrace different genres, styles, and backgrounds to enrich your creative journey.

Collaborative Endeavors: Franklin actively collaborated on various projects, from scientific experiments to political endeavors. His collaborative spirit amplified his impact. Likewise, on BuyBeats.com, don't view other producers as competitors but as potential collaborators. Collaborations can lead to innovative music projects and mutually beneficial outcomes.

Mentorship and Guidance: Franklin sought guidance from experienced individuals, benefiting from mentor-mentee relationships. Similarly, on the platform, don't hesitate to seek advice from seasoned producers. Mentorship can provide valuable insights, helping you navigate the complexities of the music industry.

Community Engagement: Franklin was deeply involved in his community, contributing to its betterment. Likewise, actively participate in the BuyBeats.com community. Engage in forums, share your knowledge, and support fellow creators. A thriving community enhances the overall experience and opens doors to new opportunities.

Long-Term Vision: Franklin's networks were part of a long-term vision for personal and collective growth. Apply this principle to your BuyBeats.com journey. Instead of seeking instant results, focus on building lasting connections. Your network can become a source of continuous inspiration and support.

In essence, the networking lesson from Benjamin Franklin lies in cultivating meaningful, diverse connections, fostering collaborations, seeking guidance, actively engaging in the community, and maintaining a long-term vision. As you navigate BuyBeats.com, let Franklin's approach guide you in creating a network that not only propels your individual success but contributes to the thriving community as a whole.

REVOLUTIONIZING THE FUTURE OF MUSIC PRODUCTION:

In essence, BuyBeats.com isn't just a platform; it's a revolution in the world of music production. It's a departure from the conventional, a leap into a future where music producers are not just earners but architects of their destiny. Your journey on BuyBeats.com is a testament to the changing narrative of success in the music industry.

As we conclude this chapter, ponder on this: Why BuyBeats.com? Because it's not merely a platform where you sell beats; it's a transformative force that reshapes your understanding of success. It's a commitment to your growth, a celebration of your unique voice, and a blueprint for a future where your passion for music translates into enduring prosperity.

In the upcoming chapters, we'll delve deeper into the practical aspects, strategies, and insider tips that will maximize your experience on BuyBeats.com. Get ready to unlock the full potential of your music production journey with the BuyBeats.com advantage.

Chapter 3

Your Guide to Getting Paid: Our Affiliate Marketing Business Model Revealed

In this chapter, we embark on a journey to demystify the realm of affiliate marketing, a powerful tool that can elevate your success on BuyBeats.com to unprecedented heights. Affiliate marketing, often misunderstood or overlooked, is a dynamic strategy that has been a cornerstone of success for many online ventures, and now, it's time for music producers like you to harness its potential.

Understanding Affiliate Marketing: A Comprehensive Insight

Before we get into the intricacies of how affiliate marketing seamlessly integrates with BuyBeats.com, let's explore its historical roots and significance. In 1996, during the beginning stages of e-commerce, Amazon.com, under the visionary leadership of Jeff Bezos, pioneered affiliate marketing. This groundbreaking move marked the beginning of a transformative journey, demonstrating that a collaborative approach to driving traffic and sales can be mutually beneficial. Amazon's Associates Program invited website owners to promote products, offering them a commission on each sale generated through their referrals. This innovative strategy not only empowered individual promoters but also laid the foundation for a dynamic and expansive network of affiliates.

As we draw inspiration from Amazon's affiliate marketing success story, it becomes evident that the principles that propelled their growth are universal. Amazon's program showcased the potential for businesses, both large and small, to thrive through collaboration. Fast forward to the present, and BuyBeats.com is offering a similar opportunity for mainly artists and music producers to become affiliates and contribute to the platform's growth. By joining our affiliate program, you're not just promoting beats – you're becoming an essential part of a vibrant community, where your efforts translate into meaningful streams of income. The benefits extend beyond financial gains; they encompass the satisfaction of being part of a pioneering platform that values and rewards the contributions of its members. At BuyBeats.com, we recognize the power of collaboration, and we want our affiliates to feel great about their role in driving the platform's success. Your involvement is not just about promoting beats; it's about being a vital force in the evolution of the music production landscape. Your success is intricately woven into the fabric of BuyBeats.com's prosperity.

At its core, affiliate marketing is a symbiotic relationship between content creators and platform owners. As a BuyBeats.com member, you automatically step into the realm of affiliate marketing. This means that every link provided to direct traffic to your beats is a potential avenue for additional income. The system tracks each click, each engagement, and each conversion – a level of transparency and reward seldom seen on other platforms.

LEVERAGING UNIQUE LINKS: YOUR PATH TO MULTIFACETED EARNINGS

BuyBeats.com stands out in the affiliate marketing landscape by offering you a multitude of unique links. These links are not just gateways to your beats; they are potent tools for wealth generation. As you share these links, the system meticulously tracks the origin of traffic. This tracking mechanism ensures that you are duly rewarded for every artist and producer you bring into the BuyBeats.com ecosystem.

COMMISSION SPLITS: A PROFIT-SHARING COMMUNITY

BuyBeats.com operates on a profit-sharing community model. Unlike traditional platforms where your earnings are confined to direct beat sales, our platform extends the wealth to various income streams. Let's break down the commission splits, unraveling the ways in which your efforts translate into financial rewards:

Subscription Profits: When you invite a producer or artist to sign up, and they opt for a monthly subscription, you receive a substantial 40% to 65% of the subscription fee. This is a paradigm shift from other platforms that often leave you unrewarded for such referrals.

Second Tier Subscribers: Delving deeper, the second-tier subscribers, those brought in by your referrals, contribute to your income. You receive 10% of the subscription fees generated by these second-tier members, creating a cascading effect of earnings.

Stream Revenue for Producers: BuyBeats.com introduces a groundbreaking feature – getting paid when your beats are played. If you invite a music producer to the platform, every time someone plays their beats, you receive 30% of the stream revenue payout. This is a game-changer, turning beat plays into a lucrative income stream.

Stream Revenue for Artists: When you invite recording artists, and they play your beats, you earn 50% of the stream revenue. Even when they explore and play beats from other producers, you still receive 20% of the stream revenue payout, reinforcing the value of your network.

Beat Sales Commissions: If your customers decide to explore and purchase beats from other producers on the platform, you receive 30% of the sales price. This unique approach ensures that you continue to benefit from your customer's engagement on the platform.

Direct Sales Profits: When your own customers purchase beats from you, you receive the entire sales price – a remarkable 100%. This is an exclusive advantage that BuyBeats.com offers, allowing you to retain full earnings from sales to your direct customers.

THE AFFILIATE ADVANTAGE: UNLEASHING POSSIBILITIES

Affiliate marketing, when seamlessly integrated into your journey on BuyBeats.com, opens a realm of possibilities. Imagine a scenario where every click, every share, and every engagement becomes a source of income. Let's explore the potential scenarios that showcase the transformative power of affiliate marketing on BuyBeats.com:

Scenario 1: Building Residual Income with Subscriptions

You invite a fellow producer to join BuyBeats.com, and they decide to subscribe to the platform. Every month, as they renew their subscription, you earn a substantial percentage of the subscription fee. Now, picture this scenario unfolding not just with one referral but with a network of producers subscribing and contributing to your continuous income stream.

Scenario 2: Beat Plays Becoming Revenue Streams

As you invite music producers to the platform, every beat play becomes a source of income. Whether it's your beats or those of the producers you referred, each play contributes to your earnings. This unique feature transforms the act of sharing beats into a lucrative venture, making your role as an affiliate marketer more rewarding than ever.

Scenario 3: Diversifying Income with Stream Revenue

Recording artists, drawn in by your links, explore and play beats on BuyBeats.com. The platform ensures that you earn not only when they play your beats but also when they engage with beats from other producers. This diversification of income streams creates a robust financial ecosystem where your network's activities contribute to your success.

Scenario 4: Retaining Customer Loyalty

Your unique links don't just direct traffic; they establish a connection that extends beyond direct sales. Even if your customers choose to explore and purchase beats from other producers, you continue to receive a significant commission. This retention of customer loyalty ensures that your efforts in bringing users to the platform yield lasting rewards.

AFFILIATE MARKETING SUCCESS STORIES: A SOURCE OF INSPIRATION

The world of online marketing is rife with success stories of individuals who have transformed their lives through affiliate marketing. Picture this: entrepreneurs, much like yourself, leveraging their networks, sharing links, and earning substantial incomes. What sets BuyBeats.com apart is the integration of this proven success model into the music production landscape.

THE LOGICAL POINT: WHY LIMIT YOUR EARNINGS?

Here's a logical point to ponder: If you're already directing traffic to your beats on other platforms without reaping the rewards that BuyBeats.com offers, why not maximize your efforts and tap into all available income streams? The unique combination of selling beats and participating in an affiliate program is a winning formula, propelling you towards unparalleled success.

In the next chapter, we'll delve into actionable strategies to optimize your unique links on BuyBeats.com, providing you with a roadmap to amplify your affiliate marketing success. Get ready to explore a world where every click, every share, and every engagement transforms into a source of continuous prosperity.

CHAPTER 3 LOGICAL POINTS

The Currency of Relationships:

Logical Point: In traditional beat-selling platforms, your relationship with customers ends with a one-time sale. On BuyBeats.com, every customer you bring becomes a long-term asset. Why settle for a single transaction when you can nurture ongoing relationships that pay dividends over time?

Beyond the Beat:

Logical Point: Other platforms focus solely on beat sales, limiting your revenue to a single source. BuyBeats.com, with its diversified income streams, allows you to earn not just from beat sales but also from plays, subscriptions, and referrals. Why confine yourself to a linear model when you can tap into multiple avenues of income?

Time-Tested Resilience:

Logical Point: The traditional model relies on immediate results, pushing producers to quit if success isn't instantaneous. BuyBeats.com advocates for a resilient, long-term approach. Why chase fleeting success when you can build a robust foundation that stands the test of time?

Your Network, Your Wealth:

Logical Point: Most platforms treat users as individuals, missing the opportunity to turn them into assets. BuyBeats.com recognizes the power of community building, transforming each user in your network into a continuous source of income. Why go it alone when you can turn your network into your wealth?

Transparent Prosperity:

Logical Point: Many platforms keep their earnings model shrouded in mystery, leaving producers uncertain about their income. BuyBeats.com, with its transparent commission splits, ensures you know exactly how you're rewarded for your efforts. Why settle for ambiguity when you can have clarity and a fair share of the profits?

Comparison to Ponder:

When weighing these logical points against the competition, it becomes evident that BuyBeats.com not only embraces innovative concepts like leverage, residual income, and community building but also provides a clear roadmap to sustainable success. Why stick with platforms that follow outdated models when BuyBeats.com offers a logical and rewarding path to prosperity?

Chapter 4

Setting the Stage for Your Success on BuyBeats.com

Before we embark on the journey of setting up links and promoting your beats, let's lay a solid foundation on BuyBeats.com. Success on this platform is not a given; it requires effort and strategic planning. Let's explore the critical elements that can make or break your success as a producer.

RECOGNIZING THE IMPORTANCE OF QUALITY

Your beats won't sell themselves. The quality of your beats is the linchpin of success on BuyBeats.com. The platform provides a vibrant community offering valuable feedback through the Beat Battle system and the forums. Engage with fellow producers, seek input, and refine your production skills. The BuyBeats.com community is a treasure trove of insights; tap into it to elevate the standard of your beats.

Thankfully, BuyBeats.com offers a free plan for producers to explore the system. However, this plan is not a recipe for success; it's a glimpse into the platform's tools. To position yourself for success, go beyond exploration. Start by uploading a substantial catalog of beats—aim for 20 to 30 high-quality productions. This isn't just a showcase; it's your portfolio, a collection that represents your unique style and versatility.

Furthermore, understand the power of beat plays. You get paid 50% of the stream revenue payout each time an artist plays your beats. With only a few beats, your earnings potential is limited. To maximize success, upload as many high-quality beats as you can. The goal is to have artists flock to your profile, creating a steady stream of income through beat plays.

LICENSING STRATEGIES FOR MAXIMUM IMPACT

Once your beats are ready for the spotlight, it's time to strategize your licensing options. Recognize that there's a buyer for every level, and BuyBeats.com empowers you with diverse licensing choices. Don't limit yourself; offer a range of licenses to cater to different needs and budgets.

Standard Lease: This is the entry level. Set a reasonable price, perhaps $15 to $20, with specific limitations on usage. It's an excellent option for those with budget constraints.

Premium Lease: Move up the ladder by offering a premium license at a slightly higher price, around $25 to $35. Provide additional perks such as both MP3 and WAV file versions for more flexibility.

Tracked Out Version: Upsell with a tracked-out version, offering stems for each track in your beat. Set a higher price, maybe between $50 to $150. Serious artists seeking more control in the studio will find this appealing.

Unlimited Lease: Upsell to offer an Unlimited License version, offering stems for each track in your beat. Set a higher price, maybe between $150 to $200 or more. Provide additional perks such as both WAV. and/or Tracked Out file versions for more flexibility. Serious artists seeking more control in the studio will find this appealing.

Exclusive Beat: Charge $250 or more for exclusivity; once purchased, the beat is off the market. This option appeals to artists seeking sole exclusive rights to use the beat.

Customize your licenses to match the unique flavor of your beats. Provide options that cater to various needs and budgets, giving buyers the flexibility to choose what aligns best with their requirements.

CRAFTING YOUR BUYBEATS.COM IDENTITY

Your producer profile is not just a placeholder; it's the cornerstone of your digital identity on BuyBeats.com. Before diving into your promotion and marketing, cultivate a profile that reflects your dedication and professionalism. Let's explore the key elements that will elevate your BuyBeats.com presence and set the stage for success.

VISUAL IMPACT: THE POWER OF A PROFILE PICTURE

Your profile image is the initial handshake in the vast digital realm. It's not merely a visual embellishment; it's the gateway to building trust and relatability. Whether you opt for a sleek logo or a friendly photo, make it count. Studies emphasize the impact of human faces in forging connections, so consider using a personal image to add to that human touch.

The visual component is your chance to leave a lasting impression. Choose a high-resolution image that aligns with your brand and style. This isn't just about aesthetics; it's about creating a sense of familiarity and approachability for potential collaborators and buyers.

CATALOG DEPTH: BUILDING A MUSICAL PORTFOLIO

Your beat catalog is the digital inventory that invites potential buyers into your creative universe. Quantity and variety are your allies in this realm. While the free plan allows exploration, serious producers recognize the power of a comprehensive catalog. Aim for 20 to 30 beats to showcase your versatility and provide potential buyers with a rich array of choices.

Consider your beat catalog as a dynamic portfolio. Regularly update it to keep your offerings fresh and engaging. Cover various genres and moods to cater to a broad audience, making your profile a one-stop destination for diverse musical needs.

TYPE BEATS: BRIDGING THE GAP WITH FAMILIARITY

In a sea of beats, standing out is an art. The "Type Beats" strategy serves as a bridge of familiarity in the vast musical landscape. By associating your beats with well-known artists, you provide a quick understanding of the style and vibe. This visual shortcut aids potential buyers in identifying beats that align with their artistic vision.

Create associations with popular artists for your beats. Incorporate celebrity images that resonate with the beat's style. Use clear and concise descriptions to enhance understanding. This approach not only simplifies the browsing experience for buyers but also adds a layer of authenticity to your offerings. Same concept goes for naming your beat titles.

COMMUNITY ENGAGEMENT: BUILDING ALLIANCES

BuyBeats.com isn't merely a marketplace; it's a thriving community of music producers. Actively engage with fellow producers, participate in forums, and contribute to beat battles. Beyond the transactional aspect, building relationships within the community enhances your visibility and opens doors for collaborations and valuable feedback.

Join forums and immerse yourself in discussions. Provide constructive feedback on beat battles. Follow and engage with other producers to foster a sense of camaraderie. The collaborative spirit of the community can propel you beyond individual efforts, creating a network that supports and amplifies your journey on BuyBeats.com.

PROFILE COMPLETENESS: A SIGNAL OF SERIOUSNESS

A fully filled-out profile signals your commitment and seriousness as a producer. Leaving sections blank might convey a lack of engagement or dedication. Treat your profile completeness as a testament to your professionalism.

Fill out all relevant sections of your profile. Provide a concise yet informative bio. Include links to your social media or external portfolios. Each element contributes to a holistic representation of your producer identity. This completeness not only aids potential buyers in understanding your offerings but also positions you as a committed and serious contributor to the BuyBeats.com community.

As you embark on this BuyBeats.com adventure, remember that success is not just about selling beats; it's about building lasting connections. Your profile is the first step in making a positive impression and standing out in this thriving marketplace.

The Beat Quality Quandary:

Logical Point: Beats on BuyBeats.com require proactive efforts for success. The chapter underscores the importance of quality standards and highlights the community's role in providing constructive feedback. Producers are urged to leverage this community support for elevating the quality of their beats.

The Essence of Catalog Building:

Logical Point: BuyBeats.com's free plan is an introduction, not a strategy for success. The chapter stresses the need for a substantial beat catalog (20 to 30 beats) to attract consumers and generate revenue through beat replays. A broader catalog ensures diverse preferences are catered to, increasing the potential for more listeners and income.

Licensing Mastery:

Logical Point: The chapter introduces licensing as a pivotal element in a producer's success. Offering beats at various levels (standard, premium, unlimited, tracked out, and exclusive) allows producers to cater to a spectrum of buyers, ensuring flexibility in their purchasing choices and broadening their audience.

Crafting a Captivating Profile:

Logical Point: An engaging avatar or profile image is highlighted as an essential element for producers. Whether it's a personal image or a logo, it serves as a visual introduction. The chapter suggests that a personal image adds a human touch, establishing a connection with potential buyers.

Community Engagement:

Logical Point: The chapter underscores the importance of community engagement. Producers are encouraged to step into forums, participate in beat battles, and forge alliances. The narrative emphasizes the value of collaboration and relationship-building within the BuyBeats.com community.

Chapter 5

Mastering Your Dashboard for Lasting Success

In this chapter, I'm going to explore the heart of your experience on the platform – your dashboard. Dive into your dashboard—a user-friendly hub where you control the reins of your BuyBeats.com experience. It's your go-to place for managing beats, monitoring your income, and unlocking the full potential of what the platform offers to you.

DASHBOARD: YOUR KEY TO MARKETING SUCCESS

As with any substantial platform, BuyBeats.com comes equipped with a robust members area called the "dashboard." Don't let the wealth of information overwhelm you; after this chapter, you'll be navigating it like a pro. It's important to note that the mobile app may have limitations compared to all the features available in the dashboard. For a comprehensive understanding of what is available, ensure you explore the dashboard on a desktop.

I also want to mention that the dashboard has a bunch of stuff I won't go into much detail about because it's pretty easy to figure out. Like, there's the "My Beats" tab where you manage your beats, which is kind of a standard feature on any beat platform. Same goes for some other features and links in the dashboard—they're pretty straightforward.

My main goal here is to point out the things that'll help you get started with marketing and understand the important stuff about promoting links. Most of the tools I'll talk about in this chapter are the ones you really need to know for your marketing journey.

1. MARKETING TOOLS SECTION

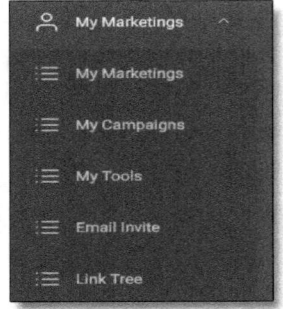

Your "My Marketing" Tab

On the left panel of your dashboard, you'll find the "My Marketing" tab. This section is a treasure trove of tools designed to enhance your reach and impact. Let's break down what you'll discover here:

A. MY CAMPAIGNS - STRATEGIC CAMPAIGNING FOR SUCCESS

Under "My Campaigns," you'll encounter a tab for setting up campaigns to track your links. These campaigns are your secret weapons, allowing you to track the effectiveness of each link. We provide unique campaign codes for this purpose, empowering you to identify your most fruitful promotional strategies.

HERE'S THE PROCESS:

To begin, click the "Add New" button on the top right of the campaign page. Once you're on that page, you'll find a list of pages where you can add a unique code. This code helps track various metrics, such as link hits, clicks, sign-ups, and even provides a percentage breakdown of unique clicks.

Share	Click	Unique Click	Signups	Conversion Rate	Created Date	Action
Share	260	192	2	1.0%	09-06-2023 02:21 AM	View / Delete
Share	1	1	0	0.0%	07-25-2023 01:51 PM	View / Delete

Let's break it down with an example. If I want to send people directly to BuyBeats.com's homepage and track my results, I'd use a link like this: https://buybeats.com?cid=Mzg2. This coded link with the extra **"?cid=Mzg2"** extension added to the link not only informs the system that I'm the one driving the traffic but also credits me when the user signs up.

On the dashboard's campaign page, you can check statistics like unique clicks, total clicks, sign-ups, and the conversion rate. This tracking system allows you to evaluate the effectiveness of your links and determine if they're worth the effort.

For instance, let's say you plan to share a link in your Instagram bio. Instead of a generic "Go to BuyBeats.com to check out my beats," try a more strategic approach. In your video or description, encourage users to click the link in your bio for specific content like a beat, sound pack, sample pack, etc. The link in your bio, customized with your unique code (e.g., buybeats.com?cid=Mzg2), ensures smarter marketing and better results. You can even use different link codes to track the effectiveness of various campaigns. Maybe you want to know which platform is getting more clicks from FaceBook, Twitter, Tik Tok, Instagram, or even from your emails or blogs. It's all designed for you to make smart marketing decisions.

Now, for many other pages besides the homepage where you could use your link, your username becomes the unique identifier of who sent the traffic. For example, buybeats.com/fatfingers — if that link is used, the system will know that Fat Fingers, who is me, sent the customer. The same applies if I use the following link, our system will recognize that it's me who sent the traffic.

(buybeats.com/fatfingers/freetraining)

However, if I want to get more detailed to understand where the traffic is coming from, let's say I'm going to post that link in 10 different places on the internet like my blog, Instagram, Facebook, my own website, etc. I can then come to the "My Campaign" section and create 10 different tracking codes. For example, I will have link 1 for my Instagram bio and then have link 2 for my TikTok bio.

Link 1 -
https://buybeats.com/FatFingers/freetraining?cid=Mzg4

Link 2 -
https://buybeats.com/FatFingers/freetraining?cid=MzC5

The (**?cid=Mzg4**) and (**?cid=MzC5**) added to the link is the unique code generated to track where your visitors are coming from when directed to the same location. You can create as many tracking codes as you need to track all your traffic sources, which is extremely important if you run paid ads.

Remember, never just direct someone to BuyBeats.com; always use your links provided by the system, ensuring your username is embedded and optionally using tracking on various campaigns.

B. MY MARKETING - TRACKING TRIUMPHS: YOUR MARKETING ANALYTICS

Under the "My Marketing," tab you'll find your marketing page, you'll observe the incoming traffic from various link sources. This straightforward tool allows you to monitor the traffic you're receiving and identify the latest clicks from your links and campaigns. Whether you directed people to your profile page or attached a campaign ID, you can review the logs right here. This page also provides insights into the number of unique clicks you've received.

Understanding what unique clicks are is crucial. Unique clicks represent the first time a person from a specific IP address interacts with our system. If they click the link five times, only one instance is considered a unique click.

At the top right, you'll find several links with your username in them. Additionally, there's a direct link to access all of your links in "My Tools." section which we will discuss next. It's all about keeping you informed on the success of your marketing efforts.

C. MY TOOLS - CRAFTING SUCCESS: YOUR TOOLKIT UNVEILED

Navigate to the "My Tools" tab to access a toolkit tailored for your success. Here, discover not just links but also email samples, banners, and scripts ready for use in private messages or social media outreach. These tools are crafted to elevate your promotional game.

YOUR LINKS:

The cornerstone of your marketing efforts lies in the "Links" tab. Here, you'll find a collection of URLs crucial for promoting your beats and the affiliate program. These links are your key to attracting traffic, and we'll go deeper into their power in phase 2.

Beyond your regular username (e.g., buybeats.com/fatfingers), which also is an affiliate link, multiple affiliate links lead visitors to different sales pages and information about our opportunity.

Note "Your-Username" in these samples will be replaced with your actual username.

General Invite Page

https://buybeats.com/Your-Username/invite

The general invite link is tailored for both artists and producers. Leverage these links to expand your network and bring more individuals into the BuyBeats.com community.

This link explains the Beat Play Commissions

https://buybeats.com/Your-Username/aboutbeatplaysinvite

PRODUCER INVITES LINKS

https://buybeats.com/Your-Username/freetraining
https://buybeats.com/Your-Username/producerinvite

These links are a goldmine for producers. It leads to video presentations providing comprehensive insights into what BuyBeats.com offers. Use these links to introduce fellow producers to the platform effortlessly.

Artist Invites Link

https://buybeats.com/Your-Username/mobile

Mobile App Link Page

https://buybeats.com/Your-Username/mobile

Your Pro Store Link

https://buybeats.com/pro/Your-Username

Link Tree Management Link:

https://buybeats.com/Your-Username/links

This Free Book (eBook version)

https://buybeats.com/Your-Username/freebook

Manage various links in one place, directing users to Instagram, TikTok, your website, blog articles, Cash App, or PayPal. The link has your username, ensuring credit even if users sign up later.

Your Banners: For websites or blogs, use embedded banners to enhance visitor experience.

Your Scripts: Pre-written scripts are available for text messages or private messages. Engage in permission marketing by starting conversations and building rapport before offering information or links.

For example, with producers, inquire about their struggles, and gradually introduce the idea of trying a new system like BuyBeats.com, emphasizing it pays whether sales are made or not. For artists, express interest in their work, inquire about their preferences, and slowly introduce your beats, seeking their opinion first.

The key is to build rapport before sending links or information. Even if users sign up to listen to your beats without making a purchase, you still get paid.

D. EMAIL INVITE: STREAMLINED OUTREACH: THE POWER OF EMAIL

The email invite is straightforward. After obtaining someone's email, choose from various subject lines and body texts provided. Select a pre-written script, and the email will appear to come directly from you with your chosen content. This feature simplifies the process of reaching out to potential collaborators or clients.

Navigate to the "My Tools" tab to access a toolkit tailored for your success. Here, you'll find not just links but email samples, banners, and scripts ready for use in private messages or social media outreach. These tools are crafted to elevate your promotional game.

E. LINK TREE - CENTRALIZING LINKS: YOUR PATH TO VISIBILITY

One of the jewels in our crown is the Link Management system. Similar to services like Link Tree, it's a one-stop-shop for compiling multiple links in one place. We offer this to you for free, saving you money compared to other platforms.

2. MY CUSTOMERS

Within your dashboard, the "My Customers" section allows you to view and manage the artists and producers who signed up under your name. This feature provides valuable insights into the activity of your customer base, helping you understand which producers and artists are active and paying members.

Moreover, the "My Customers" section enables direct communication with your customers. You can send messages, introduce yourself, offer assistance, or even explore collaboration opportunities. These customers are not just names on a list; they are individuals contributing to your success on the BuyBeats.com platform.

BONUS OFFERS

Right below the same tab, you'll find the "Bonus Offers" section—an often-overlooked treasure trove for producers on the site. This section allows you to entice new customer growth by offering digital products or packs as bonuses. For instance, you can create a post on social media platforms like Instagram, promoting a gigabyte of sample sounds that you're giving away for free to anyone signing up at BuyBeats.com through your link.

3. MY INCOME

Another crucial area within your dashboard is the "My Income" section. Here, you can meticulously track all your sales from beat sales and subscriptions. Additionally, the "My Play Income" section allows you to keep tabs on your play income and provides a platform for requesting payouts once you meet the set threshold, currently standing at $10.

When you achieve this threshold, you'll receive a notification, signaling that you can withdraw your earnings. For added convenience, if your play income reaches $30 and you haven't initiated a withdrawal request, the site will automatically process the payment and send it directly to your PayPal account.

Within the "My Income" section, you gain insights into your subscriptions, detailing how many customers have paid you for the month. At the top, a quick chart review allows you to visualize your performance over the past several months.

It's important to note that beat payouts or beat sales are tracked every 15 days, offering a brief overview at the top of your "My Income" page. On the other hand, subscriptions are paid out monthly, with the last and most previous payouts visible in the overview.

Switching to the "My Play Income" section, you can not only view your recent payouts but also search for specific time periods. This feature enables you to perform detailed checks on how much you were paid during particular intervals.

In summary, the "My Income" tab serves as a comprehensive tool for monitoring and managing all the income you receive on the platform. It provides a clear picture of your sales, subscriptions, and play income, empowering you to stay on top of your financial performance and make informed decisions about your earnings on BuyBeats.com.

This strategic approach not only attracts new users but also positions you as a valuable resource within the platform. The bonus offers act as a lead generation tool, bringing in users who can be contacted for potential collaborations or additional offerings. The "Bonus Offers" section is a powerful tool to leverage your creative assets for both immediate and long-term gains on BuyBeats.com.

CONCLUSION

As we journey through this manual, we'll delve even deeper into the intricacies of links and their role in your success. Remember, the more you understand, the more you can leverage the power of BuyBeats.com to build a thriving career in music production. Don't be the producer who overlooks these tools – embrace them and watch your success unfold.

Chapter 5 Logical Points
Smart Link Tracking:

Logical Point: Unlike other platforms where link tracking is an afterthought, BuyBeats.com empowers you with detailed campaign tracking tools. By strategically utilizing unique campaign codes, you gain insights into the effectiveness of your marketing efforts. Why settle for blind promotion when you can make informed decisions based on real data?

Holistic Marketing Approach:

Logical Point: While some platforms focus solely on beat sales, BuyBeats.com provides a comprehensive marketing toolkit. From campaigns and links to email invites and banners, the platform equips you with diverse tools. Why limit yourself to a single avenue when you can craft a multi-faceted marketing strategy?

Data-Driven Decision Making:

Logical Point: BuyBeats.com doesn't leave you guessing about the success of your campaigns. The dashboard provides statistics on unique clicks, total clicks, sign-ups, and conversion rates. Why rely on assumptions when you can make informed decisions based on concrete data?

Network Amplification:

Logical Point: Traditional platforms treat users in isolation, missing the potential for community-based success. BuyBeats.com recognizes the value of building a network and turning it into a continuous source of income.

Why go solo when you can leverage the power of your network for lasting prosperity?

Transparent Tools for Success:

Logical Point: While many platforms keep their promotional tools hidden or complex, BuyBeats.com offers transparent access to links, email samples, banners, and scripts. Understanding and using these tools becomes a straightforward process, eliminating unnecessary confusion. Why struggle with opaque systems when clarity is readily available?

Strategic Link Deployment:

Logical Point: Instead of generic links, BuyBeats.com encourages strategic link deployment. Customized links with unique codes ensure you receive credit for the traffic you generate. Why settle for a standard approach when you can tailor your links for maximum impact and results?

Link Tree Management:

Logical Point: Managing various links can be chaotic on other platforms. BuyBeats.com simplifies this with the Link Tree, allowing you to direct users to multiple destinations seamlessly. Why juggle multiple links when you can consolidate them for a smoother user experience?

Long-Term Prosperity Mindset:

Logical Point: BuyBeats.com promotes a long-term approach to marketing, encouraging you to build rapport before sharing links. This not only enhances the user experience but also contributes to sustained success. Why opt for short-term gains when you can cultivate lasting relationships for continuous income?

Comparison to Reflect:

When comparing these logical points against other platforms, it becomes evident that BuyBeats.com doesn't just offer a dashboard; it provides a strategic command center for your marketing endeavors. The emphasis on data, community, and transparency sets it apart, offering a logical and rewarding path to sustainable success. Why adhere to outdated marketing practices when BuyBeats.com presents a forward-thinking and effective approach to maximizing your music production career?

Chapter 6

Boost Your Residual Income Gains with the Blue Share Buttons

As you navigate through BuyBeats.com, you'll find a common feature—the distinctive blue share buttons scattered across the site. These buttons are more than mere links; they're personalized with your unique username. This customization transforms every shared link into a valuable asset, creating unparalleled opportunities for long-term customer acquisition and residual income. Whether you're sharing a blog post, a captivating beat, or a curated playlist, each interaction becomes a potential source of ongoing revenue. Let's delve into the mechanics of how this dynamic system works.

THE POWER OF YOUR BUYBEATS.COM PROFILE'S BLUE SHARE BUTTON

When setting up your BuyBeats.com user profile, don't overlook a powerful tool—the blue share button located at the top right. This feature is unique to each user, enabling you to share a producer's beats effortlessly.

Imagine you're on Facebook, and an artist in a Facebook group is on the hunt for R&B beats. The problem is you don't really make R&B beats. Well, don't worry! You could seize this opportunity. As a logged-in user, you can visit any producer's profile, click on the blue share button, and generate a link personalized with your username. Now, when you share this link on Facebook or any other platform, it's not just a link—it's a gateway to open up an income stream for yourself. You now just promoted another producer in which when the artist signs up and listens to the beats you shared and possibly purchases any, you get paid. The great thing is, they can come back multiple times and no matter how much time in between, you still get paid for their activity. You can't beat that! No pun intended.

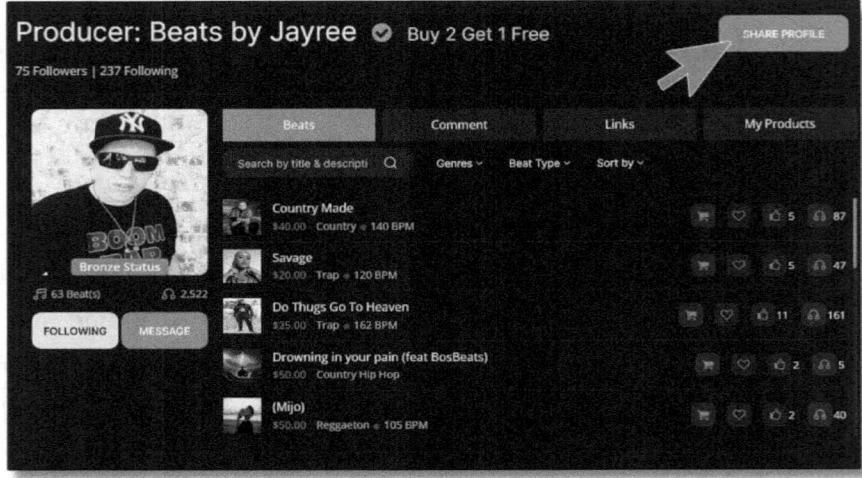

You must understand that the magic begins when someone clicks on your shared link. They land on the producer's profile, and every action they take becomes a potential source of income for you. If they sign up, congratulations—they're now your new customer. Any beats they purchase or listen to contribute to your earnings for a lifetime.

Here's the breakdown: You receive 20% of streaming revenue every time an artist plays a beat if they signed up through your link. If this newfound customer decides to make a purchase, you pocket a substantial 30% of the sale. It's a win-win scenario, benefiting both you and the producer whose beats you promoted.

So, whether you're a producer or an artist, leverage the blue share button on producer profiles to expand your network, increase your earnings, and make the most out of your BuyBeats.com experience.

FROM PRODUCTS TO PROFITS: BLUE SHARE BUTTON'S IMPACT ON DIGITAL OFFERINGS

As a valued member of BuyBeats.com, you possess more than just the ability to create beats—you have the opportunity to curate and share a diverse array of digital products. From compelling eBooks to innovative sample packs and various digital treasures, the platform's online store feature opens exciting avenues for promotion and income generation.

Here's how it works: Once you delve into the world of BuyBeats.com, you can explore the option to upload digital products. Whether they are experts in crafting insightful eBooks or creating captivating sample packs, this platform empowers users to monetize their unique skills.

Upon successfully uploading a digital product, the platform equips you with the tools to promote and share it effectively. The familiar blue share button, a constant companion across BuyBeats.com, becomes your key ally. By clicking this button, you generate a unique link, seamlessly tied to your username. This link serves as a direct bridge between the shared content and potential customers.

Now, let me reiterate this point again. When fellow members or enthusiasts click on it and explore BuyBeats.com, every action they take, whether it's purchasing a digital product, listening to beats, or subscribing, contributes to your income. The brilliance of this system lies in its simplicity: the blue share button transforms into a promotional tool, allowing users to attract customers and generate income through various activities on the platform.

Navigate to the online store, conveniently located in the site header, to explore a centralized hub showcasing a myriad of digital products. This not only enhances the visibility of creators' offerings but also provides potential customers with an accessible way to discover and engage with the content.

In essence, the digital products feature and the online store at BuyBeats.com empower you, as a member, to transform your promotional efforts into a potent source of income. Seize the opportunity, hit that blue share button, and let these digital products become a beacon, attracting customers and establishing a pathway to long-term residual income.

USING BLUE SHARE BUTTONS FOR PLAYLIST RESIDUALS

At BuyBeats.com, playlists take on a unique role, providing users with a platform to curate and share their favorite beats. This feature not only adds a personalized touch to the user experience but also opens doors for a compelling opportunity—thanks to the distinctive blue share button that accompanies each playlist.

Let's dive into how this works: As a member, whether you're an artist or a producer, you can create your playlist by simply hitting the red button inside the player. This action allows you to add beats of your choice, tailoring the playlist to your preferences. The versatility of this feature enables users to showcase not only their own creations but also the beats that resonate with them.

Now, here comes the exciting part. The blue share button, a consistent presence across BuyBeats.com, plays a crucial role in transforming your playlist into a potential source of income. Clicking this button generates a unique link with your username embedded in it. Share this link across your social networks, community groups, or with your audience.

When someone clicks on your shared link and decides to sign up on BuyBeats.com, they become your customer. From that point forward, every action they take on the platform contributes to your residual income—whether it's buying beats, listening to them, subscribing, or engaging in any other monetized activity.

The beauty of the playlist feature lies in its community-centric approach. BuyBeats.com encourages collaboration and mutual support among users. When you share a playlist, you not only showcase your musical taste but also contribute to the collective success of the community. This cooperative spirit is further enhanced by the affiliate program, allowing others to promote and generate income from your beats.

In summary, the playlist feature on BuyBeats.com is more than just a collection of beats—it's a dynamic tool for expression, collaboration, and income generation. So, don't forget to hit that blue share button and turn your playlist into a gateway for acquiring customers and creating a lasting stream of residual income.

BEYOND WORDS: LEVERAGING BLUE SHARE FOR LIFELONG GAINS

The Blog Post feature on BuyBeats.com is a powerful tool that allows users to access and share valuable insights, updates, and information directly from the platform. What makes this feature even more compelling is the inclusion of the blue share button—a tool that turns each blog post into a potential source for lifelong customer acquisition and residual income.

Imagine this scenario: You're scrolling through BuyBeats.com and come across a well-crafted and insightful blog post, created by the platform itself. As you read through the content, you notice the blue share button prominently placed. Clicking on this button generates a unique link tied to your username.

Now armed with this link, you can effortlessly share the blog post across various platforms such as Facebook, Twitter, or other social media channels. The link directs your audience straight to the blog post on BuyBeats.com. The magic happens when they engage with the content.

As they read the blog post, captivated by the insights and ideas, the platform recognizes their visit as originating from your shared link. If they decide to sign up, you've just facilitated a new customer acquisition. The benefits don't stop there—every time they play a beat or make a purchase or subscribe, you receive credit for their activity, creating a continuous stream of income.

This feature is not just about sharing content; it's about leveraging the creativity and knowledge presented on BuyBeats.com. The blog post becomes a gateway, providing valuable content and serving as a catalyst for others to explore and engage with the platform.

So, the next time you come across an insightful blog post on BuyBeats.com, don't forget to use the blue share button. It's not just a share button; it's a key to unlocking opportunities for customer acquisition and residual income, creating a symbiotic relationship between shared content and financial success.

BEATS, BATTLES, AND REFERRALS: THE TRIPLE WIN OF BLUE SHARING

Another exciting aspect of BuyBeats.com is the Beat Battle Arena. It's a space where intense battles unfold, showcasing the incredible talent within our community. We've witnessed some legendary showdowns, and in recognition of the participants' skills, we've actually distributed thousands of dollars in prizes to the winning producers.

The Beat Battle Arena features a distinctive blue share button. When you share a beat battle using this button, it works its magic. It generates a unique link, incorporating your username. Anyone who clicks on this link is redirected straight to the heart of the battle action. For those who appreciate the thrill of a good beat battle, it's an invitation to enjoy the excitement.

This isn't just about sharing the joy of music; it's also a fantastic opportunity for you. By utilizing the blue button, you're not only spreading the word but also earning credit for every new signup that comes through your shared link. So, whether you're an active participant in the battles or a keen spectator, sharing the experience can earn you more than just applause. Imagine saying, "Check out this battle – the winner takes home $25, $100, $500 or even $1500! Join in, and if you like what you see, sign up." They might just become your newest referral, contributing to your lifetime residual income. It's a win-win for everyone involved.

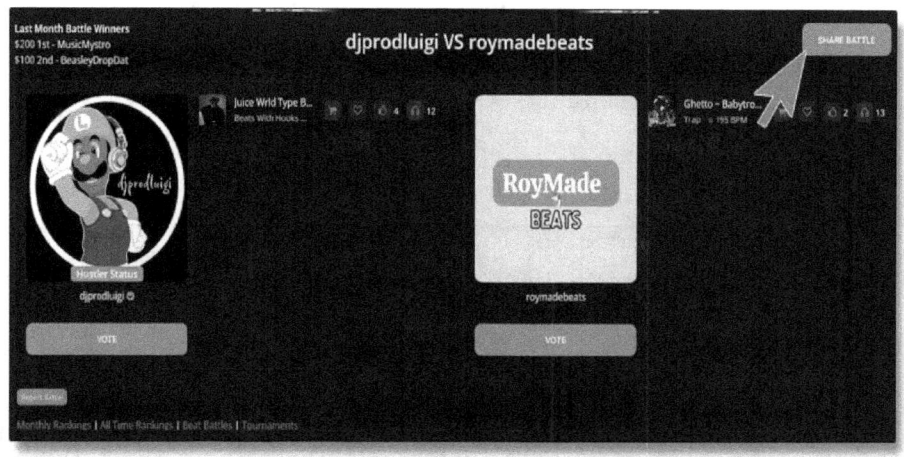

BUILDING BRIDGES: BLUE SHARE BUTTON AND BEAT REQUEST COLLABORATIONS

The Beat Request Page on BuyBeats.com is a valuable resource, featuring a prominent Blue Link that you can share. This page allows artists to make specific beat requests from the talented producers in our community. Let me break down the concept using the blue button and its significance. Artists use this page to articulate their beat preferences, and here's where it gets interesting.

Imagine a fellow producer sharing an artist request using the blue share button. For instance, they might say in a FaceBook group, "Hey, if any of you create trap beats, there's an artist on BuyBeats.com looking for exactly that." This single share could lead to a remarkable outcome – it has the potential to bring in multiple new producers to the platform. Don't underestimate the power of sharing these requests!

Often, producers might hesitate, thinking, "I don't typically produce that style of beat." However, this shouldn't discourage you from utilizing the blue share button. By sharing the request and the unique link it generates, you're not just helping fellow producers discover opportunities; you're also creating a pathway for them to become your customers. When these producers sign up after clicking your link and engage with the platform, you begin to generate a lifetime of residual income.

This process reinforces the collaborative and community-driven spirit of BuyBeats.com, where everyone has the potential to thrive together. So, the next time you come across an artist request, seize the opportunity, hit that blue share button, and watch as you open the door to a stream of potential customers and long-term income.

SHARING KNOWLEDGE, BUILDING INCOME: THE BLUE SHARE BUTTON METHOD

The How-To Video Page on BuyBeats.com is a goldmine of information, providing insights into the intricacies of the platform, its various features, and offering valuable guidance. Notably, on these pages, you'll discover the presence of the blue share button – again, a feature that can significantly enhance your experience on the platform and contribute to your financial success.

Imagine this scenario: As you explore the How-To Video Page, you notice the blue share button. By clicking this button, you generate a unique link. Now, armed with this link, you have the power to introduce other producers to the wealth of information available on the platform. You might say something like, "I stumbled upon a page that explains everything about gaining more customers as a music producer. Check it out using this link – you won't believe what you've been missing!"

Sharing this link serves a dual purpose. First, it intrigues other producers, encouraging them to explore the platform's features and understand its potential. Second, it provides you with a means to generate residual income. As those producers sign up and engage with the platform, you earn credit for their new sign-ups, creating a continuous stream of income. This sharing process is not just about promoting the platform but also about empowering fellow producers to make informed decisions. It's a win-win situation – they gain valuable insights, and you, as the inviter, benefit from their engagement on BuyBeats.com.

So, the next time you're on the How-To Video Page, don't overlook the blue share button. Utilize it to share knowledge, spark curiosity, and set in motion a cycle of residual income that benefits both you and your fellow producers.

Logical Points for Chapter 6: Boost Residual Gains with Blue Share Buttons

1. **Personalized Residual Income:**

   Logical Point: While other platforms may offer basic sharing options, BuyBeats.com's blue share button provides a personalized touch. Every shared link is uniquely tied to your username, turning each interaction into a potential source of ongoing revenue. Why settle for generic sharing when you can have a customized gateway to long-term income?

2. **Diversified Income Streams:**

   Logical Point: Unlike platforms focused solely on one type of content or transaction, BuyBeats.com leverages the blue share button across various features. From beat sales to digital products, playlists, and blog posts, this diversified approach maximizes your earning potential. Why limit yourself to a single revenue source when you can tap into multiple avenues using the same blue share button?

3. **Community-Driven Prosperity:**

   Logical Point: BuyBeats.com emphasizes community collaboration, where each shared link contributes not only to your income but also to the success of the entire platform. The blue share button isn't just about personal gains; it's a tool for building a thriving community. Why go solo when you can actively contribute to and benefit from a supportive network?

4. **Transparent Earnings Model:**

Logical Point: Unlike platforms that leave producers in the dark about their earnings, BuyBeats.com ensures transparency with clear commission splits. The blue share button isn't just a tool; it's part of a system where you know exactly how your efforts are rewarded. Why settle for uncertainty when you can operate in a transparent environment and receive a fair share of the profits?

5. **Strategic Long-Term Approach:**

Logical Point: BuyBeats.com promotes a strategic, long-term mindset, emphasizing the cumulative impact of shared links over time. The blue share button isn't just about immediate gains; it's a key to building a lasting stream of residual income. Why chase short-lived success when you can invest in a sustained and thriving future?

Comparison to Ponder: When comparing these logical points to other platforms, it's evident that BuyBeats.com stands out by combining personalization, diversification, community focus, transparency, and a strategic approach. The blue share button becomes more than a feature; it becomes a symbol of a platform that not only offers innovative earning opportunities but also provides a clear roadmap to sustainable success. Why settle for platforms that lack these essential elements when BuyBeats.com offers a logical and rewarding path to long-term prosperity?

Chapter 7

Embrace Additional Key Features Tailored for Your Success on BuyBeats.com

In this chapter, I want to highlight the invaluable aspects of some additional key features offered on BuyBeats.com. Many producers may not fully grasp the extensive benefits that come with our platform, making it crucial to shed light on the features designed to elevate your experience on the platform.

The brilliance of our referral program lies in the subscription referrals. For every artist or producer that subscribes through your referral link, you receive a substantial commission ranging from 40% to 65% of the subscription fee. What's truly remarkable is that after referring just three premium artists or producers to the platform, your earned percentage can cover your monthly membership cost. This means you don't have to dip into your pocket, as the income generated from your referrals essentially cancels out your monthly membership fee.

Consider the contrast: On other platforms, producers may pay $15 to $20 per month, and that cost comes directly out of their own funds. At BuyBeats.com, our system is designed to empower you to make money through referrals, providing a unique opportunity to not only cover but potentially exceed your monthly membership costs. The simple task of referring three people can transform your

BuyBeats.com experience, making it a financially sustainable endeavor.

So, if you're a premium member, embrace the power of our referral program. Share the benefits of BuyBeats.com with your network, refer artists and producers, and unlock a pathway to financial independence within the platform. Your journey on BuyBeats.com becomes not just a creative venture but a strategically lucrative one, driven by the potential of our profit-sharing model.

REFERRAL STATUS

Take a look at our site, and you might notice some members with different statuses on their profile images. Achieving different referral statuses not only showcases your dedication but also indicates that your monthly membership is covered by the income generated through your referrals. Currently, for premium plan subscriptions, you receive the following commission rates:

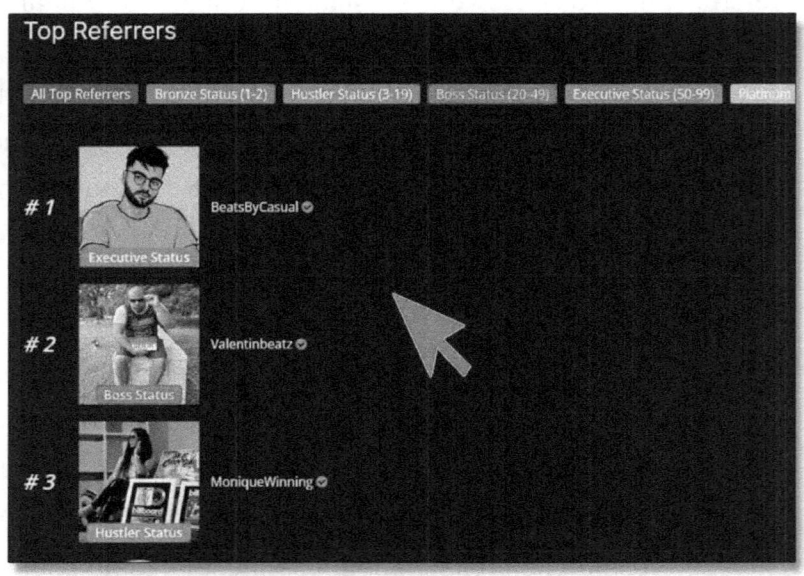

Bronze Status: 40% ($6.00) 1-2 Active Subscribers
Hustler Status: 40% ($6.00) 3-19 Active Subscribers
Boss Status: 50% ($7.50) 20 - 49 Active Subscribers
Executive Status: 60% ($8.99) 50-99 Active Subscribers
Platinum Status: 65% ($9.75) 100 plus Active Subscribers

These percentages represent the commission you earn from the $14.99 monthly payment for premium plan subscriptions. As you progress in statuses, the commission rates increase, reaching up to 65% for Platinum Status with 100 or more subscriptions. This unique structure allows you to tailor your efforts and earnings based on your referral success.

FOLLOW SYSTEM

When you explore your profile on BuyBeats.com, you'll notice the presence of follow buttons, a feature akin to those found on popular social media platforms. However, the significance of these follow buttons on BuyBeats.com goes beyond conventional social media interactions.

Encourage fellow artists, particularly those interested in your beats, to click the follow button. By doing so, they not only become part of your audience, but they also set themselves up to receive essential notifications. These notifications serve as a direct line to your updates, ensuring that every time you upload new beats, your followers are promptly informed.

As a producer, leveraging the follow system becomes a strategic move. When you engage with your social media audience, consider prompting them with a call to action: "Make sure to follow me on BuyBeats.com for the latest updates on my beat uploads!"

This simple yet powerful step ensures that your audience stays engaged and up to date with your latest musical creations.

But the advantages don't end there. Your followers not only receive notifications when you upload beats but also when you post in the forum. Imagine dropping a new product, providing an update, or sharing valuable insights outside of your beat uploads. Your followers get instant notifications, keeping them connected with your overall journey on BuyBeats.com.

Building a substantial following on BuyBeats.com is more than a number – it's a strategic move to ensure ongoing visibility and traffic to your beats. So, as you continue to produce and share your beats, encourage your audience across various platforms to click that follow button on BuyBeats.com and stay in the loop for all your latest updates. This not only fosters engagement but also enhances your reach within the vibrant community of BuyBeats.com.

BEAT REQUEST

Now, let's delve deeper into the Beat Request system, a powerful feature that serves music producers in a unique way. Upon using the Beat Request system, artists undergo a verification process. If they are confirmed as an artist, a distinctive blue check is added next to their name on our platform. This verification process ensures that you are engaging with real artists.

Once an artist completes the criteria for the type of beats they are looking for, our system notifies all relevant producers. This dynamic process eliminates the need for producers to search for artists actively seeking beats. Instead, artists are coming to you. The beauty of this system is that it not only streamlines the connection between artists and producers but also provides an excellent opportunity for visibility and sales.

Imagine receiving notifications about beat requests tailored to your expertise. Responding to these requests allows you to showcase your beats directly to artists who are actively seeking your style. This not only enhances your visibility but also increases the likelihood of selling your beats to artists genuinely interested in your sound.

As you explore the website, take a moment to check out the beat requests. You'll notice that some artists are not just looking but are actively purchasing beats. The platform keeps a record of the number of beats artists have purchased, giving you valuable insights into potential sales opportunities.

In essence, the Beat Request system is designed to be a win-win for both artists and producers. Artists find the beats they need effortlessly, while producers get direct exposure to potential customers genuinely interested in their musical style. So, don't hesitate to engage with the Beat Request system, submit your beats, and leverage this unique feature to enhance your visibility and sales on BuyBeats.com.

BEAT FEED

Now, let's dive into the Beat Feed feature, a powerful tool to keep your audience engaged and informed about your latest beats. Similar to popular social media platforms, the Beat Feed ensures that every time you upload new beats, they appear in the feeds of your followers. This straightforward yet effective concept allows your audience to stay up to date with your music, fostering continuous engagement.

Imagine your followers scrolling through their feeds on BuyBeats.com, and there, prominently displayed, are the beats you've recently uploaded. This feature acts as a direct channel to your audience, providing them with instant access to your latest creations. Whether you're experimenting with new sounds, dropping a beat that's been highly anticipated, or simply maintaining a consistent upload schedule, the Beat Feed ensures that your audience remains plugged into your musical journey.

So, make the most of this feature by regularly uploading your beats, keeping your followers in the loop, and capitalizing on the direct visibility the Beat Feed provides. It's a simple yet powerful way to maintain an engaged audience and maximize the impact of your beats on BuyBeats.com.

BEAT BATTLES

Now, let's delve into the exciting world of Beat Battles on BuyBeats.com. This feature, often overlooked by many producers, offers a unique opportunity to showcase your skills, compete with fellow producers, and even win attractive prizes.

Every month, there's a chance for producers to claim first and second place prizes in the Beat Battles. The payout is currently based on the determined income, and to rank in the top five, you need to have over 5 beat battles a month. The ranking system takes into account your scores, wins, losses, and rating percentages.

Picture this: as a producer on BuyBeats.com, you have the chance to stand out among your peers, earn recognition, and potentially win cash prizes. The monthly ranking system ensures that producers who consistently deliver high-quality beats and actively participate in the platform are rewarded for their efforts.

Stay tuned for special events and tournaments, as they occasionally feature substantial cash prizes. The announcement area in the forum is where staff share information about these events, so be sure to keep an eye out for opportunities to take your Beat Battles experience to the next level.

In essence, Beat Battles add an exciting layer to your journey on BuyBeats.com, offering not only a platform to showcase your skills but also a chance to be rewarded for your dedication and talent. So, gear up, participate, and let your beats make a statement in the vibrant world of BuyBeats.com Beat Battles.

BEAT PACKS

During the writing of this book, a user request led to the creation of a beat pack feature. This feature enables you to bundle multiple beats together for sale. This feature reflects BuyBeats.com's commitment to enhancing its platform based on user input.

To use this feature, access your beat management tab, where you'll find it. Create a name for your beat pack, and if desired, add artwork. Define the license terms for the pack; however, please note that each pack can have only one license type, such as standard or premium, etc. To make your beat pack visible on the platform, ensure you have at least four beats in it.

Users seeking beat packs can visit the store link, where they'll find the beat pack section, showcasing producers offering these bundled deals. You will soon be able to offer the beat backs from your profile page. As BuyBeats.com continues to evolve, this feature will grow and adapt to user needs, providing a valuable tool for offering multiple beats at a single price.

FREE PROMOTION WITH OUR ADVERTISING NETWORK

If you take a moment to glance at the banners near the bottom of the site, just above the footer, you'll notice the names of several producers alongside the number of beats in their profiles. This exclusive feature is reserved for premium producers – an advertising network displaying these producers' names and the quantity of beats they have to offer. The best part? It's a complimentary feature on the BuyBeats.com platform.

Let me explain how you can get your banner circulating around the site. I just discussed with you how the beat battles on the platform work. One crucial element for beat battles is votes. This leads to a hidden benefit in voting on other producers' battles – every time you support them with a vote, you earn impressions for your ads.

Here at BuyBeats.com, you don't have to pay for your banner ads to be seen on the website. Instead, you simply vote on other music producers' beat battles. By doing so and supporting your peers, you accumulate ad impressions, ensuring your banner circulates around the site. It's a win-win situation – beneficial for those who vote and equally advantageous for those seeking votes in their beat battles.

Go ahead, give it a try now, and observe how many ad impressions you receive for actively participating in beat battles. It's a simple yet effective strategy to boost your visibility on the platform.

PRO STORES

As a BuyBeats.com member, you have access to an exclusive feature called Pro Stores, providing you with a unique opportunity to self-brand and further customize your presence on the platform. Pro Stores come at no additional cost and offer a range of benefits for producers looking to enhance their visibility and collaboration opportunities.

With Pro Stores, you can not only customize the header to align with your branding but also add other producers to your store for joint promotion. Imagine having your own space to showcase your beats while also featuring beats from other producers you admire or wish to collaborate with. This collaborative approach not only strengthens the sense of community but also creates opportunities for mutual growth.

For example, you can have your beats showcased in a store that's exclusively yours, but you can also include beats from other producers you want to promote. This way, you're not only promoting your beats but also contributing to the success of fellow producers. It's a win-win scenario that fosters collaboration, networking, and potential income through shared exposure.

FEATURES AND BENEFITS FOR RECORDING ARTISTS ON BUYBEATS.COM:

In this final section of the chapter, I want to outline what recording artists receive on BuyBeats.com. It's essential for you, as a music producer, to understand precisely what is offered to recording artists on our platform. This knowledge will enable you to highlight the most important points and values when communicating with artists.

One significant perk for artists is that when they sign up and get verified, indicating that we have confirmed their status as an artist, they receive a blue check, symbolizing their verified artist status on the platform. Moreover, each time an artist plays beats on the platform, they earn stream revenue just for listening to beats. This groundbreaking feature benefits artists while they explore thousands of beats, and it's crucial to convey this information when prospecting.

As mentioned earlier, artists have the option to upgrade to a premium account on BuyBeats.com. Here's what they gain: any artist with a premium account receives a free standard beat once a month. They receive a credit in their account, usable at any time to download a standard beat priced at no more than $25. This credit is automatically applied as they pay their monthly subscription, with no timeframe for its use.

Artists interested in the referral program can participate by having a premium account, enjoying the same benefits as music producers. Additionally, artists can set up a ProStore with a premium account, specifying the type of producers they want to purchase beats from. The advantage is that, instead of someone else earning a commission, artists can receive a 30% cashback on all beats purchased from their own ProStore. This feature only applies if the artist has a premium account.

Furthermore, artists earn a 40% commission on all subscriptions they refer, and this percentage can increase based on the number of premium plan referrals they bring to the platform. Again, just like music producers, artists on BuyBeats.com can obtain a premium account and enjoy the same rewards as music producers. It's a platform where both creators and artists thrive together.

CLOSING OF THE CHAPTER

This concludes phase one of our guide, where we delved into numerous features and benefits offered on the BuyBeats.com platform. The focus was particularly on shaping the mindset required to thrive in this unique program. It's worth noting that a program like BuyBeats.com has never been offered to music producers before, signifying that we are collectively breaking new ground in the realm of earning income.

Now equipped with knowledge about the system and BuyBeats.com's offerings, the next phase will concentrate solely on building up your customer base – a pivotal step in reaping the rewards of this great system. While this guide covers a comprehensive set of features, it's important to note that we're continually adding updates and new features to enhance the platform further. In the event that significant additions are made post-publication, we will provide supplementary information to ensure you stay informed and equipped to make the most of the evolving community.

Without further ado, let's dive into phase two, where we will discuss key strategies to grow your customer list and embark on the journey of building your residual income as a music producer on BuyBeats.com.

Phase 2

Growing Your Customers on BuyBeats.com

Every day on BuyBeats.com, when I witness new users signing up, I can't help but affirm to myself that the system is working. Some customers join through my affiliate links, making it a beautiful day. Equally gratifying is when other producers and artists sign up new customers under their name. Seeing someone else benefit when a new user signs up under them is a testament to the success of the platform. It's not just me making money; it's the collaborative effort of artists and producers being rewarded in this profit-sharing community.

THE PROSPECTING JOURNEY: LEARNING TO DELIVER THE MESSAGE

Before the official launch of BuyBeats.com in April 2022, I embarked on a journey in March to find 20 people who believed in the system. Little did I know that in the process of prospecting, I would gain invaluable experience in delivering the message and talking about the program. This early experience forms the foundation of what I'll be teaching in this phase, and it's a testament to the power of hands-on learning.

DISCOVERING THE BUYBEATS.COM ADVANTAGE: UNIQUE SELLING PROPOSITION

Confidence played a crucial role during these early days. I was confident that BuyBeats.com offered a unique concept unparalleled in the music production community. Let me break down precisely what sets us apart—our Unique Selling Proposition.

At BuyBeats.com, we are not just a beat platform; we are a revolutionary force in the music production industry. Unlike any other beat platform, we pay our users streaming revenue, sharing 20 to 50% of the streaming profits with them. No one else is doing this for music producers. We go further by compensating recording artists for beat plays. Imagine earning money for simply listening to beats—that's the BuyBeats.com advantage.

What's more, we stand alone by splitting our subscription fees with our users. While other companies absorb all subscription fees, we pride ourselves on giving back to our users a remarkable 40 to 65% of those subscription fees. This isn't just a platform; it's a community invested in your success.

THE POWER OF PRESENTATION: CONVEYING YOUR MESSAGE EFFECTIVELY

I'll discuss the importance of presentation here in phase two, emphasizing that how you present your offer to prospects and leads can make or break their interest. A strong presentation is key to capturing attention and convincing potential users of the value BuyBeats.com brings to the table.

INSIGHTS FROM PROSPECT TO MENTOR: NAVIGATING THE BUYBEATS.COM COMMUNITY

While I'll touch on successful strategies employed by other users, I'll also share my personal journey, focusing on what worked during the initial stages of building BuyBeats.com. Presentation is everything, and in this phase, we'll explore how to present your offer effectively to both prospects and leads, particularly targeting music producers and recording artists.

BELIEVE IN YOUR SUCCESS: INSIGHTS FROM MENTORS

Believing in the unique opportunity we have and the success of existing producers on the site is crucial. Everyone progresses at their own pace, and in the upcoming chapters, I'll share insights from my mentors about achieving goals steadily over time. Success is about persistence and sustainable growth.

Consider this introduction as a prelude to the upcoming chapters in Phase Two. Let's embark on this journey together and explore the strategies, insights, and wisdom that will contribute to your success on BuyBeats.com. Without further ado, let's get into it.

Phase 2: Logical Points
Understanding Your Unique Selling Proposition (USP):
Logical Point: Knowing BuyBeats.com's USP empowers you to influence customers effectively. By understanding the distinctive features—such as revenue-sharing, diversified income streams, and transparent commissions—you can communicate tangible value to potential users.

Maximizing Income Opportunities:
Logical Point: The phase 2 introduction highlights that BuyBeats.com offers more than just beat sales. By comprehending the income potential from plays, subscriptions, and referrals, you logically see the advantage of tapping into multiple revenue streams. This knowledge positions you to optimize your earnings.

Embracing Long-Term Success:
Logical Point: The emphasis on resilience and a long-term approach logically guides you away from the pitfalls of seeking immediate success. Instead, it encourages you to build a sustainable foundation for enduring prosperity, recognizing that success in the music industry is an ongoing journey.

Harnessing the Power of Community:
Logical Point: Acknowledging the community-building aspect on BuyBeats.com logically reveals the potential to turn your network into a continuous source of income. Instead of navigating the journey alone, you can leverage the collective strength of the community for mutual success.

Seeking Clarity for Prosperity:

Logical Point: The mention of transparent commission splits logically encourages you to seek clarity about how your efforts are rewarded. By understanding exactly how you benefit, you can make informed decisions and confidently engage in the platform, knowing your fair share of the profits.

Making Logical Choices for Prosperity:

Logical Point: When considering these facts, it becomes evident that BuyBeats.com presents a logical and rewarding path to prosperity. By logically comparing these points against other platforms, you are prompted to make informed choices based on the innovative concepts and transparent structure offered by BuyBeats.com.

Chapter 8

Building Your Social Media Presence for Success

Alright, buckle up because in this chapter, we're diving deep into the strategies that pave the way for success. But before we plunge into the details, let's set the tone and give you a glimpse into what it truly means to be a partner with buybeats.com.

As a member of buybeats.com, you're not just another face in the crowd or a mere affiliate; you're a valued partner. Let's make it clear: you're not just a statistic. You're a partner who helps steer the path of buybeats.com. Your success isn't just about you; it's connected to the journey we're all on together.

It's a distinctive role that goes beyond the transactional nature you might find on other platforms. Here, you are a business partner, someone who not only contributes to our community but also reaps the rewards alongside us.

In this chapter, I want you to see yourself not just as an affiliate marketer but as a business partner and associate. The strategies I'm about to share are not mere techniques; they are tools for partners like you to take ownership, connect with your audience, and offer valuable assistance.

Being a partner means your success is our success. Your journey is our journey. So, as we jump into relationship marketing and lead generation, envision this chapter as a guide from a friend, a colleague who wants to empower you to take the steps needed to showcase buybeats.com to those who need it.

And remember, while I primarily use Instagram, the strategies and principles discussed here are applicable across all platforms. So, whether you're engaging on Instagram, Twitter, Facebook, TikTok, or any other social media platform, you can tailor these approaches to fit your audience and maximize your impact.

Before we plunge into the nitty-gritty, let's talk about the different marketing approaches you'll be delving into to build up your customers on buybeats.com, get ready for a targeted and strategic deep dive into the realm of customer growth.

YOUR INSTAGRAM BIO!

When I started out on Instagram, one of the first things I focused on was studying how to effectively put my bio in place. They offer you a space for a bio where you can particularly stand out. Instagram, for instance, allows you to have a bio description as well as a link in the bio. This is one of the major highlights of the Instagram bio, giving you the opportunity to have a call to action (CTA) and actually have a message there, driving traffic to the link outside of the videos you post.

In my videos, you often hear me say, "Link in the bio," and I track all those link clicks in my bio. We have campaigns that we use on the platform, and I've shared with you a bit about the campaigns that include videos on our platform to guide you on setting up your campaign codes. This helps me know how many people hit on my Instagram bio.

Speaking of putting the bio together, let's discuss what you should say in your bio. Since we're attracting music producers and artists, let's look at what our company bio currently says:

COMPANY INSTAGRAM BIO:

"We are the first PROFIT SHARING Music Production community to PAY both Artists and Music Producers for Beat Plays and more. Become an Affiliate Today!"

And this is the link I use:

buybeats.com/fatfingers/links

In my bio, I mention that we're unique as a profit-sharing music production community, paying both artists and music producers for beat plays and more. The target audience is artists and music producers, so I've abbreviated our unique selling proposition in a way that is compelling to them. I also have a call to action, saying, "Become an Affiliate Today." I might even consider changing it to "Sign up for free today" to see if it gets more clicks. The key is to have a call to action (CTA), guiding your audience on what to do.

Now, let's talk about the link. Instead of just a generic link, I use buybeats.com followed by my username and /links. This links to our link management system, where I can include multiple links, each with its own title. This is a powerful tool because, even if someone doesn't click on the links in the link manager immediately, our system tracks them when they visit the link, and I still get credit if they sign up later.

So, when engaging with others on Instagram, my bio stands out. It shows that I have something unique to offer, and I'm targeting a specific audience. Remember that your bio is the first thing people see, so make it compelling and tailored to your target audience.

Now, let's explore some bio samples to spark inspiration for crafting your own:

Sample Bio's

1. Crafting Captivating Headlines:

Your bio's initial line acts as a headline, instantly seizing attention. Construct a headline that captures the spirit of your music production community or artistic voyage. Aim for intrigue, sparking curiosity.

Example: "🚀 Profit-sharing hub for Artists & Producers! Earn for every beat play. Join us and turn your music passion into rewards! 🎵 💰 #MusicProfitHub"

2. Inspiring Call to Action (CTA):

A compelling bio includes a clear call to action, guiding your audience on the next steps. Whether it's an invitation to join, sign up, or explore further, an effective CTA prompts engagement.

Example: "✨ Beats that matter, earnings that count! Profit-sharing for Artists & Producers. Turn your passion into rewards. Ready to amplify your music journey? 🚀 🎧 #MusicAmplified"

3. Strategic Hashtags for Visibility:

Elevate your reach with strategic hashtags. Integrate relevant tags resonating with your music niche. This not only organizes your content but also enhances discoverability among a wider audience.

Example: "💡 Empowering Artists & Producers! Pioneer in profit-sharing music production. Earn for each beat play. Turn your passion into earnings! 🚀 🎵 #MusicEarnings"

4. Personalized Touch:

Infuse your bio with personality, be it through emojis, a unique phrase, or a glimpse into your creative ethos. Adding a personalized touch renders your bio more relatable and human.

Example: " 🎶 Unleash the potential of your beats! Profit-sharing powerhouse for Artists & Producers. Earn for each beat play and beyond. Kickstart your music prosperity! 🎧 💰 #MusicRewards"

5. Leveraging a Link Management System:

Harness the potency of your bio link. Utilize a link management system to dynamically showcase different facets of your music journey. Even if immediate clicks don't occur, the system tracks visits, ensuring sustained connection.

Example: " 🎧 Beats that pay! Join the profit-sharing revolution for Artists & Producers. Every beat play counts. Ready to turn your beats into earnings? 🎵 💸 #MusicRevolution"

Feel free to use or modify these samples to suit the specific details and tone.

SOCIAL MEDIA BRANDING: CRAFTING YOUR PRESENCE

When joining social media networks, simplicity is key, especially when creating your username. Opt for a straightforward and memorable name. Avoid unnecessary characters or variations.

A simplistic name not only streamlines your brand but also enhances recall. I recall back in 2012 when Instagram was gaining traction, I registered and grabbed the name @BuyBeats. I secured the username, foreseeing its future importance, and didn't start using the account until a few months before we launched buybeats.com. Your username is your brand's first impression, so make it count.

For effective branding, choose a username that resonates with your brand and is easy for prospects to remember. Trust me, artists and producers won't forget "@BuyBeats." It becomes a powerful recall tool in your prospecting journey.

Now, let's discuss your profile image. A clear shot is essential, especially if you're frequently on the move. It's surprising how many interactions I come across with profiles lacking a recognizable image. If it's not a logo, ensure your personal photo is clear and identifiable. Your profile picture is often the first thing people notice, and if it's engaging, it creates a sense of familiarity. Interactions become more personal and friendly when people can connect a face to the comments. People will click on your image, returning to explore your profile further.

Remember, your social media presence is your digital identity. Crafting a cohesive and memorable brand starts with a simple and impactful username and an identifiable, clear profile image. These elements lay the foundation for meaningful interactions and successful prospecting on social media platforms.

POST DIVERSITY: STRATEGIC POSTING ON SOCIAL MEDIA

Before launching into your prospecting journey, ensure your profile showcases at least 10 posts, laying the groundwork for meaningful engagement. Our inaugural post featured me and my son, Sensei Jay, creating a comparison video between BuyBeats.com and Beatstars.com. This foundational video, prominently displayed on our Instagram page, marked the inception of our engagement and marketing endeavors.

Subsequently, we shared diverse content spotlighting the advantages of the BuyBeats.com platform, infusing purpose and personality into our profile. We recognized the need to go beyond mere beats, providing our audience with a multifaceted experience. This commitment to variety became evident in our posts.

One notable addition to our content was a video featuring a guy named Hugo, succinctly explaining the essence of BuyBeats.com in just 60 seconds. These diverse posts offered visitors valuable insights into the platform's unique features. It's crucial to create a profile that goes beyond beats, infusing personality and diverse content to ensure your profile remains dynamic and engaging.

Observing Instagram metrics, we have over 3,000 followers. However, in the last 30 days, an impressive 14,500 people engaged with our content, underscoring the significance of profile visits over sheer follower count. A well-rounded and engaging profile with good content can attract a broader audience. Our follower base primarily comprises targeted music producers and artists, emphasizing the quality over quantity of followers.

Now, I've come across some social media influencers who proudly display their impressive engagement statistics – 50,000, a hundred thousand, even half a million. It's all possible! Achieving these numbers requires a tremendous amount of dedication, and the possibilities are truly endless. We're only scratching the surface, utilizing this account and not fully maximizing its potential because there's a lot to pay attention to. However, even in the early stages, we're seeing the benefits of gaining new customers every day from Instagram alone. If you haven't already, I strongly recommend getting started and recognizing the tremendous opportunities that await.

In recognizing the significance of varied content, I've noticed some producers solely upload beats only, potentially limiting their profile's appeal. I advocate for a diverse array of content, including studio pictures, behind-the-scenes shots of beat-making sessions, discussions about production techniques, and other engaging elements. This not only makes your profile more interesting but also provides a comprehensive snapshot of your creative journey, appealing to a wider audience.

Now, with these key elements in place on your profile, you're well-prepared to dive into the realm of prospecting. It's time to shift your focus from setting up your profile to crafting effective prospecting strategies. This phase involves actively seeking out and engaging with artists and producers, initiating conversations, and guiding them to explore what BuyBeats.com has to offer. Remember, the mindset here is crucial – you're not selling; you're helping.

Approach each prospect with the intention of providing value, introducing them to a solution they may not be aware of, and addressing potential needs they haven't yet discovered. It's about guiding them toward a product that can genuinely benefit them, tailored to your target market of artists and music producers. Get ready for an exciting journey of connecting, persuading, and showcasing BuyBeats.com as a valuable resource.

As we embark on this path, keep in mind that these engaged customers will play a pivotal role in building your residual income. So, let the prospecting begin! In the upcoming chapter, we'll delve into effective strategies for finding, engaging, and converting potential customers. Stay tuned for more insights and actionable steps to enhance your prospecting game.

Chapter 9

A Blueprint for Genuine Connections and Endless Prosperity

Don't Spam! Straight out of the gate, let me make this crystal clear. It's not just unnecessary; it's counterproductive. The techniques and training laid out in this book are designed to obviate the need for such tactics. Following this guidance, your prospects are likely to approach you, seeking more information. No spam, just stimulation, engagement, and the prospect arriving where you want them – receptive to the value and information you have to offer. Period!

Now that we've got the anti-spam sentiment established, let's dial it back a notch. No more threats; I trust you're on board steering clear of the spam zone. But, in all seriousness and with a sprinkle of humor, let's dive into this chapter. I'm loading it up with tips to not only attract prospects but also to get their permission – some call it permission-based marketing.

PERSONAL TOUCH ON INSTAGRAM

When it comes to prowling Instagram for prospects, my go-to account is my personal one – catch me at @fatfingersNY. Why? Well, @Buybeats.com does its job with likes and comments, ensuring information is readily available for return visits. But for that personal touch, I'm all about my personal Instagram account. It adds a dash of intimacy to the engagement, making the connection more personal.

Now, let's delve into the Instagram landscape. With billions of users, pinpointing your target market requires a bit of strategy and insight. Fortunately, you're about to gain just that. Get ready to learn how to locate and engage with your target audience effectively.

POWER OF HASHTAGS

One powerful approach is delving into hashtags. By searching and following hashtags, you open the door to a wealth of insights. Here's why it matters: Music producers often label their beats with hashtags, offering a direct link to their identity or the specific audience they're trying to reach. Hashtags, in essence, tell a story about the poster. The same holds true for recording artists. Whether it's #unsignedartist or #newmusicalert, these hashtags provide a peek into the artist's world.

DEMOGRAPHIC HASHTAGS GUIDE

To help you navigate this terrain, I'll provide you with a comprehensive list for both demographics. This guide will give you a clear picture of what hashtags are commonly used when these creative minds share their posts. Armed with this knowledge, you'll be strategically positioned to connect with your target audience.

Music Producers	Recording Artists
#ProducerLife #BeatsForSale #Instrumentals #StudioFlow	#UnsignedArtist #NewMusic #MusicIsLife #IndieMusic

#BeatMaker	#RecordingArtist
#MusicProduction	#MusicMonday
#ProducersCorner	#Songwriting
#BeatMakersUnite	#Vocalist
#ProducerGrind	#MusicDiscovery
#ProductionLife	#SingerSongwriter
#NewBeats	#UnsignedTalent
#MusicProducer	#StudioSession
#StudioVibes	#IndependentArtist
#BeatStars	#MusicPromo
#ProducerCommunity	#ArtistsOnTheRise
#ProductionFlow	#RecordingSession
#MusicBiz	#VocalsOnPoint
#SoundDesign	#MusicRelease
#BeatCatalog	#OriginalMusic
#ProducerJourney	#MusicJourney

You can compile a list of hundreds of hash tags that artists and music producers. You are sure to find more than enough of them to engage with.

ENGAGING WITH CONTENT

Harnessing the power of hashtags is a key tactic – Instagram allows you to follow hashtags, ensuring that any content using those tags pops up in your feed. However, if impatience strikes and waiting for these tags doesn't suit you, dive into the Instagram search. You'll encounter two options: "popular posts" with hashtags, offering a mix of recent and older content, and the "recent" tab, providing content posted by Instagram users within seconds. This presents an ideal chance to both like and comment on fresh posts.

AUTHENTIC ENGAGEMENT

Authenticity is paramount in your approach. Imagine setting a daily goal of engaging with 20 or 30 posts – a reasonable endeavor. As you peruse content, particularly from music artists, avoid sounding robotic. Many fall into the trap of using automated responses, easily discernible as such. Instead, seek something unique in the content – be it a picture or a video – and open a genuine discussion by asking the right questions. These curiosity-driven queries signal to the user that you're a human genuinely interested in their post.

CONNECTING WITH ARTISTS

Take music, for instance. If an artist is releasing new music, listen to it. Comment on specific elements – praise the hook, highlight the intriguing introduction. Express your genuine interest and let them know you've followed them. Following the introduction, offer constructive feedback. For instance, propose expert feedback before they release more songs. This approach communicates that you're not there to take away; rather, you're invested in contributing to their artistic journey.

ADDING VALUE

Beyond feedback, offer valuable tips on their posts. If the graphic accompanying their music is grainy, inquire if they designed it and suggest tools to enhance graphics. This imparts value and sets the stage for reciprocity. Musicians often operate in a self-centric world, focused on taking rather than giving. By offering advice or sharing information, you stand out as someone willing to contribute, fostering a sense of mutual benefit.

This engagement strategy isn't exclusive to artists; it extends seamlessly to engaging with music producers. Utilize similar principles and hashtags, and if you're a producer hearing another's beats, provide positive critique. If a beat could benefit from a better mix or has a too-loud snare, delicately suggest improvements. This initial engagement lays the groundwork for virtual friendships.

PROMOTION AND COLLABORATION

Engagement isn't just about giving compliments; it's also about offering promotion. Ask the producer if you can reshare or repost their music on a separate Instagram account dedicated to promoting and reposting beats. This costs you nothing but can significantly benefit them. Even proposing to create a page promoting exceptional producers can lead to positive engagement.

BUILDING DEDICATED PLATFORMS

In an upcoming chapter, I'm going to talk about creating platforms, blogs, websites, or social media accounts that are dedicated to the target market you're trying to reach. Building these hubs strategically allows you to swoop down with your offer while benefiting the community simultaneously. For instance, you can build a Facebook group dedicated to producers and mixing tips or create an Instagram account showcasing producers going live in the studio or featuring hot beats. These accounts and groups can amass followings of like-minded music producers, creating a groundwork for your lead generation.

ENCOURAGING COLLABORATION

Moving beyond promotion, encourage collaboration. Platforms like BuyBeats.com facilitate collaborative efforts by allowing up to four collaborators on a beat. When a collaborative beat sells, the earnings are distributed among collaborators according to predetermined percentages. While this feature isn't revolutionary, it emphasizes the importance of how tools are utilized.

PROPOSING COLLABORATION BENEFITS

When proposing collaboration to a prospect, make clear the benefits of joining BuyBeats.com. Stress that signing up is free and explains the potential for income generation through various streams – from subscriptions to beat sales. Highlight the power of collaboration, not just in creating music but also in building a network that can lead to sustained income.

EVOLUTION OF ROLES

As you bring artists and producers into your network, your role doesn't end – it evolves. These individuals become friends with benefits, generating income through subscriptions and beat sales. By adding their beats to playlists and promoting them, you can further maximize these benefits. It's an intricate opportunity that requires thoughtful engagement. Take a look at the 20 bonus engagement scenarios at the end of this chapter to get further understanding on things you can do to sow seeds of reciprocity.

UNDERSTANDING BUYBEATS.COM

Before concluding this chapter, it's crucial to educate yourself fully on the features of BuyBeats.com. You can bring your connections into the fold by discussing these features. For example, if you talk to a producer and express interest in promoting their beats in your personal playlist, direct them to your DM for more information. It's essential not to reveal that it's associated with BuyBeats.com initially to ensure you receive proper credit by using your own links. This also sets the stage for a more in-depth conversation and exploration of the platform's functionalities.

How would that work? It's simple. Your comment, "Hey, I have been checking out your beats and wouldn't mind promoting your beats on my beat playlist. It costs you nothing to start and it's free promotion for you." A comment like this can raise multiple questions. Simply state afterwards, "If you're interested, DM me and I will tell you all about it."

INVESTMENT IN FUTURE CASH FLOW

In conclusion, this chapter offers profound insights into growing your engagement. Set aside dedicated time, perhaps an hour, five days a week, for prospecting sessions. Turn idle moments spent watching movies or aimless phone use into a rewarding task that builds future income. Remember, this isn't just a task; it's an investment in a future cash flow. With persistence and focus, the potential for growth is boundless. The possibilities presented here are extensive, and while there can be more to cover, what's laid out is a deep dive into initiating and nurturing engagement. The schedule you set for yourself is crucial – it's an investment in a future where your cash flow grows with each engagement.

Chapter 10

Learn The Art of Attracting Prospects to Grow Lasting Residual Income

In this chapter, we'll explore the art of attracting prospects to your offer. a skill set essential in the world of affiliate marketing. Attraction is a universal concept, present in various aspects of our lives, from personal relationships to our daily activities. For instance, consider the parallels between attracting the opposite sex and attracting your target audience for your offerings. Very Similar!

Just as in personal interactions, where being perceived as interesting and trustworthy is essential, the same holds true when attracting prospects to your offerings.

Prospecting and attracting your target market, in this case, artists and music producers, can be likened to an art form. This chapter will explore this art form, providing insights into the strategies and approaches that can enhance your ability to attract other music producers and artists effectively.

For every great relationship, there are key things that are very important or important things that have to happen before the person that you engage with feels comfortable enough to trust you or even do business with you. Following are ten things you will need to master when engaging with potential music producers and artists that can become a part of your team.

HERE THEY ARE IN NO PARTICULAR ORDER:

1. **Earning Trust:** Establishing trust with your audience is paramount.
2. **Strategic Timing:** Timing your recommendations for maximum impact.
3. **Understanding Needs:** Gain insight into the unique needs of music producers and artists.
4. **Targeted Guidance:** Offer recommendations tailored to individual preferences.
5. **Delivering Value:** Create valuable exchanges that benefit both parties.
6. **Human Connection:** Forge authentic connections by being relatable, not robotic.
7. **Fostering Genuine Relationships:** Transform one-time interactions into lasting connections.
8. **Enhancing User Experience:** Elevate the audience's journey for a positive impression.
9. **Nurturing Loyalty:** Build personal connections to cultivate loyalty.
10. **Empathetic Recommendations:** Show empathy in your advice for long-lasting impact.

Let's go deeper into all 10 points. I will show you how you can engage with your prospects to make you more attractive to them or foster a relationship where you can then set up the stage to offer your offerings.

1. BUILDING TRUST

Establishing trust with your audience is crucial. By engaging with them genuinely and consistently, you can build a strong foundation for trust. When you leave comments like these on their posts:

"Your creativity knows no bounds! Every post of yours is a masterpiece. Thanks for consistently inspiring us! 🔥 #CreativeGenius"

"I love how you share the behind-the-scenes of your process. It makes your journey feel so relatable. Keep shining!

What to Expect: Your supportive comments will likely result in the prospect feeling appreciated and valued, possibly leading to them exploring your profile or engaging in further conversations.

2. STRATEGIC TIMING

Timing matters when introducing affiliate recommendations. After engaging with your audience, you can strategically recommend products or services that align with their recent achievements or challenges. For example:

"Congratulations on your latest beat release! Your work is incredible. Have you explored ways to monetize your beat plays? It could be a game-changer for your bottom line. Let's chat more about it! 🚀 🎶 #StrategicOpportunities #MonetizingBeats"

What to Expect: Timing your recommendations based on their recent activities increases the chances of them being receptive to your suggestions and potentially exploring monetization options.

3. UNDERSTANDING NEEDS

Personalized engagement allows you to understand the specific needs of your audience. When you see a pain point, you can recommend relevant solutions:

"I noticed you mentioned the challenges with slow beat sales—it can be tough. I used to worry about that myself until I found a new platform. It's not just a place to share beats but also pays artists for listening and pays music producers for beat plays by artists. A great way to turn your passion into earnings. Let me know if you want more info or tips on maximizing it! 🎤 🎙 #SolutionFocused #Stream Revenue Boost"

What to Expect: By addressing their pain points directly, you're likely to pique their interest and open the door for further discussions on potential solutions.

4. TARGETED RECOMMENDATIONS

Knowing your audience enables you to make targeted recommendations that resonate with their preferences and interests:

"I love your passion for vintage sound equipment! If you're into that vibe, I recently came across these amazing plugins and hardware that specialize in vintage tones. They could be a game-changer for your unique style! 🎹 🔊 #MusicProducer"

What to Expect: Targeted recommendations are more likely to capture their attention and lead to discussions about how these products can enhance their music production.

5. CREATING VALUE

Providing valuable content establishes your authority and creates a foundation for more meaningful engagements:

"Improving vocal techniques is a journey, isn't it? I found this comprehensive guide on [specific topic] that really helped me. Check it out and let me know if you find it valuable too! 🎤 🎙️ #VocalTraining #ArtistCommunity"

What to Expect: Sharing valuable resources fosters a sense of gratitude and respect, often resulting in the prospect viewing you as a knowledgeable source for guidance.

6. HUMANIZING THE INTERACTION

Humanizing your brand through personal engagement makes your recommendations more relatable and increases the likelihood of audience exploration:

"Wow, I resonate so much with your journey as a music producer! It's amazing how [specific challenge] led me to discover a new platform that helps me tremendously. It completely transformed my approach. Your stories make this community feel like a family. Thanks for sharing! 🎵 #MusicJourney #CommunityConnection"

What to Expect: Personal connections humanize your interactions and can lead to deeper conversations, potentially even collaborations or mutual support within the community.

7. FOSTERING GENUINE CONNECTIONS

Personal engagement fosters genuine connections, transforming one-time engagements into long-term relationships:

"Your dedication to your craft is truly inspiring. I've seen your journey unfold, and every milestone is well-deserved! If you ever need support or advice, count on me. Let's keep this creative journey going together! 🚀 🎶 #ArtisticJourney #LoyaltyInAction"

What to Expect: By expressing your admiration and offering support, you can foster a deeper connection with the prospect, potentially leading to ongoing collaboration, mentorship, or mutual support within the creative community.

8. ENHANCING USER EXPERIENCE

Personal engagement enhances the overall user experience, creating a positive environment for introducing your offers at a later date:

"Your live streams are not just entertaining but also packed with valuable insights! 🚀 I recently tried out [specific DAW], and it's been a game-changer for me. If you ever want more details or tips, let me know. Let's keep the music conversation alive! 🎶 🔗 #MusicProductionTalk #UserExperience"

What to Expect: By enhancing the user experience through meaningful interactions, you set the stage for a receptive audience when you eventually introduce your affiliate offers, increasing the likelihood of conversion.

9. NURTURING LOYALTY

Building personal connections nurtures loyalty, encouraging prospects to choose your recommendations over others:

"Your trust and loyalty mean the world! I've got something exciting coming up that I think aligns perfectly with your style. Can't wait to share it with you first. Your support has been the driving force behind my journey! ✨ 🎵 #GratefulHeart #LoyaltyInAction"

What to Expect: Nurturing loyalty creates a dedicated following who are more inclined to engage with and choose your recommendations in the future. It can also lead to exclusive opportunities and early access to your offers.

10. EMPATHY IN RECOMMENDATIONS

Personal connections allow you to empathize with the challenges and aspirations of your audience, resulting in more empathetic and effective affiliate recommendations:

"I feel you on the slow beat sales struggle. It's not easy, but there's hope! I recently discovered a new platform, and it's been a game-changer for me. The features really address some of those pain points. Hit me in the DM so I can hook you up! 🎵 #SolutionDriven #ArtistEarnings"

What to Expect: Empathy in your recommendations showcases your understanding of their struggles and can lead to a stronger emotional connection. This, in turn, increases the likelihood of them trying out your recommended solutions.

By integrating these ten principles into your engagement strategy, you can create deeper connections, improve the user experience, nurture loyalty, and offer more empathetic recommendations, all of which contribute to the success of your affiliate marketing efforts.

As you engage with your audience and provide value, you'll set the stage for reciprocity to flourish, ultimately bringing prospects closer to you and making your offers more appealing. Continue to foster these connections and watch as they evolve into meaningful partnerships.

Chapter 11

(DM) Direct Messaging Mastery - Applying Cialdini's Principles

Direct Messaging (DM) presents a unique opportunity for personalized and persuasive communication. In this chapter, I'll explore how to engage in a conversation with a random user, applying Robert Cialdini's principles of influence to subtly guide prospects towards exploring your offer.

Back in 2007, I was introduced to Robert Cialdini's principles through a program focused on mentorship. The transformative book, "The Psychology of Influence and Persuasion," became a game-changer, reshaping my mentality when it came to persuading others to say yes to my offers. While I share these principles with you, it's essential to acknowledge that the foundation comes from Cialdini's groundbreaking work. I've been applying these principles since 2007, especially in 2008 when I introduced my sellmorebeats.com course.

In that beat selling program, I shared these same principles with producers who then shared with me their success stories about increased sales and overall improvements. These principles are timeless; they are like laws that consistently yield results. It's crucial to recognize that mastering them requires practice and study. You might not get it right the first time, but with consistent application, you'll become adept at prospecting and guiding potential clients through your offerings.

Here's an actual picture of the book, "The Psychology of Influence and Persuasion" by Robert Cialdini, in my possession since 2007. This book has been a guiding force in my journey, and the principles within have proven effective over the years. Now, let's dive into a specific principle – reciprocity. It's a universal principle that encourages people to respond positively when you offer them something of value, fostering a desire to reciprocate. I want to introduce the remaining principles to empower you  to use them effectively in your direct messages, whether you initiate the conversation or someone DMs you based on a comment you made on their post. Let's explore these principles to enhance your persuasive skills in direct messaging.

PRINCIPLE 1: RECIPROCITY IN THE DMS

Reciprocity is about initiating the conversation with a gesture of goodwill. Begin by offering something of value, such as a relevant resource, tip, or information. This sets the tone for reciprocity, making the user more inclined to reciprocate by considering your offer. Please Note: What you initially share doesn't always have to be about BuyBeats.com. Remember, you are just establishing a meaningful friendship by providing something of value.

Example 1:

You write: "Hey, I've recently come across a fantastic resource that helped me improve my beat-selling game. Would you be interested in checking it out?"

Response from Prospect: "Sure, I'd be interested."

You write: "Ok, here is the link to check it out, [Share your link and the write]. After you check them out, let me know what you think, or I will just check back in a day or two with you!

How does this principle work for you: By offering something of value, you create a sense of reciprocity, encouraging the prospect to consider your offer."

Example 2:

You write: "I've been researching ways to enhance beat production. Do you want to know a cool trick that can elevate your beats to the next level?"

Response from Prospect: "Absolutely, I'm curious!"

You write : "Ok, here is the link to check it out [Share a valuable tip or technique]. After you check it out, let me know what you think, or I will just check back in a day or two. Thanks!

How does this principle work for you: Offering a valuable tip fosters reciprocity and makes the prospect more receptive to your suggestions."

PRINCIPLE 2: COMMITMENT AND CONSISTENCY IN THE DMS

Encourage small commitments within the conversation. Start with open-ended questions that prompt the user to share their thoughts or experiences related to the topic. Once they've committed to the conversation, gently guide them towards considering your offer.

Example 1:

You write: "Hey, I've noticed your interest in music production. What's your biggest challenge when it comes to selling beats?"

Response from Prospect: "I struggle with getting noticed as a producer."

You write: "I understand. Let's explore some solutions together. **How does this principle work for you:** By prompting the prospect to engage in the conversation and share their challenges, you encourage commitment to the conversation."

Example 2:

You write: "I've been looking into beat-selling strategies. Can you share your thoughts on what's been working for you recently?"

Response from Prospect: "Well, I've been focusing on social media promotion."

You write: "Interesting! Let's dive deeper into that strategy.

How does this principle work for you: By asking for the prospect's thoughts, you prompt them to commit to the conversation and share their experiences."

PRINCIPLE 3: SOCIAL PROOF IN THE DMS

Incorporate social proof subtly into the conversation. Mention positive experiences others have had with your product or service, creating a sense of credibility and trust. This can be in the form of testimonials, reviews, or brief success stories.

Example 1:

You write: "Hi there! Some fellow producers have shared how using my beat-selling platform boosted their sales. Would you like to hear their success stories?"

Response from Prospect: "Yes, I'd love to hear some success stories."

You write: "Ok, here are some of their stories [Share testimonials or success stories]. After you check them out, let me know what you think, or I will just check back in a day or two. Thanks!

How does this principle work for you: By showcasing success stories from fellow producers, you leverage social proof to build credibility and encourage the prospect to consider your offer."

Example 2:

You write: "Hey, your music is making waves! Some artists I've worked with found my services helpful. Interested in hearing about their experiences?"

Response from Prospect: "Definitely, I'm curious."

You write: "Ok, here are a couple of their experiences [Share positive feedback from previous clients]. After you check them out, let me know what you think, or I will just check back in a day or two. Thanks!

How does this principle work for you: By highlighting the positive experiences of others, you establish credibility and trust, making the prospect more open to your suggestions."

PRINCIPLE 4: AUTHORITY IN THE DMS

Establish your authority by sharing relevant expertise or knowledge. Provide valuable insights that position you as an expert in your field. This helps build trust, making the user more receptive to your suggestions.

Example 1:

You write: "Your beats are top-notch! Having worked in production for over a decade, I've learned some groundbreaking techniques. Want me to share a few with you?"

Response from Prospect: "Absolutely, I'd appreciate that."

You write: "Ok, here are some techniques I've picked up [Share your insights]. After you check them out, let me know what you think, or I will just check back in a day or two. Thanks!

How does this principle work for you: By positioning yourself as an authority and offering valuable expertise, you establish credibility and trust."

Example 2:

You write: "Your music is impressive. I've been running a successful beat-selling platform since 2008, and I know the ins and outs of effective marketing. Would you like some tips?"

Response from Prospect: "Yes, please share your insights."

You write: "Ok, here are some tips to get you started [Share your tips]. After you check them out, let me know what you think, or I will just check back in a day or two. Thanks!

How does this principle work for you: By sharing your expertise, you position yourself as an authority, making the prospect more receptive to your suggestions."

PRINCIPLE 5: LIKING IN THE DMS

Build a likable persona through friendly and relatable communication. Use emojis, express genuine interest in the user's opinions, and maintain a conversational tone. This fosters a positive connection, making them more open to your suggestions.

Example 1:

You write: "Your style is unique and catchy. I'm working on a project and thought about collaborating with you. What do you think? Would love to chat more about it!"

Response from Prospect: "Wow, that sounds interesting! Let's discuss it."

You write: "Great! Let's explore some collaboration ideas.

How does this principle work for you: By initiating a friendly and relatable interaction, you foster a likable persona, making the prospect more open to your suggestions."

PRINCIPLE 6: SCARCITY IN THE DMS

Incorporate elements of scarcity by subtly hinting at limited opportunities or exclusive benefits related to your offer. This creates a sense of urgency without being overtly salesy.

Now that you have a deeper understanding of these principles, let's move on to the sample DM dialogues at the end of this chapter. These examples will showcase how to apply these principles effectively in your direct messaging conversations for maximum impact.

Example 1:

You write: "Hey, I've found an amazing opportunity in the beat-selling market, but it's limited. Interested in taking advantage of it before it's gone?"

Response from Prospect: "Yes, I'd like to know more."

You write: "Ok, here is the link to check it out [Share your exclusive opportunity]. After you check it out, let me know what you think, or I will just check back in a day or two. Thanks!

How does this principle work for you: By hinting at limited opportunities, you create a sense of urgency without being pushy, prompting the prospect to act promptly."

MAKE SURE YOU FOLLOW UP

Follow-Up Example 1:

You write: "Hey [Prospect's Name], I hope you had a chance to explore the resources I shared with you. I'm genuinely interested in your thoughts and whether you found them helpful. Feel free to reach out if you have any questions or if there's anything specific, you'd like to discuss. Looking forward to hearing from you!"

Follow-Up Example 2:

You write: "Hi [Prospect's Name], it's been a few days since we last chatted. I wanted to check in and see how your journey in exploring the resources is going. If you've had a chance to review them, I'd love to hear your feedback. And if you need any further assistance, don't hesitate to reach out. Wishing you all the best!"

CHAPTER SUMMARY:

In this chapter, we've delved into the art of Direct Messaging (DM) mastery, combining it with Robert Cialdini's principles of influence to engage prospects effectively. We explored the principles of reciprocity, commitment and consistency, social proof, authority, liking, and scarcity, and learned how to apply them in DM conversations to ethically guide prospects toward exploring our offers. By providing valuable content, building rapport, and subtly incorporating these principles, you can enhance your persuasive skills in DMs without coming across as pushy or sales-driven. Remember that authenticity and a genuine interest in the prospect's needs are the cornerstones of successful persuasion. In the journey of affiliate marketing, building relationships, providing value, and staying committed are keys to success. So, stay motivated, persistent, and focused on the bigger picture, as each 'yes' can lead to enduring success and passive income for years to come. Embrace the journey, celebrate victories, and keep inspiring others with your valuable solutions in the dynamic world of affiliate marketing. Here's to your continued success!

Chapter 12

Lead Generation: 21 Marketing Ideas for Music Producers to Generate Leads

Now that we've covered prospecting and different methods for engaging with your target market through comments on their posts and private messaging, it's important to understand the necessity of keeping leads flowing. The messages we share and the actions we take to signal our target market about our identity and the value we bring to their lives are crucial in maintaining and growing leads.

A significant aspect of what I've been stressing is the idea of adding value to the target market. Without this value, you risk not being perceived as a valuable resource. Now is the time to deploy resources that will guide many to our main office. Many producers may find it challenging to embrace this concept, being hesitant to give away assets. However, it's essential to grasp the analogy of putting a worm on the hook—enticing the fish before hooking them. Once hooked, you can reap the rewards.

Understanding this concept is fundamental because everything I refer to as lead magnets functions as that enticing worm on your fishing hook. Occasionally, these "worms" may slip away, much like the experience of a tug on the fishing line resulting in the disappearance of the bait. But worry not; it's part of the game. Not every signal you send out will result in a catch, and not every free offer will secure a connection. The key is to persist and keep dropping your lines; eventually, you'll land your fish.

Without further ado, in this particular chapter, I want to talk about different ways you can actually attract leads with lead magnets to bring these leads into your pipeline, eventually exposing them to the office that you have. Let's get into it.

1 - FREE BEAT GIVEAWAY:

Lead Magnet: Exclusive access to a high-quality beat or instrumental track.

I frequently come across online campaigns that vehemently reject the idea of free beat giveaways, and understandably so. Many producers invest significant time and resources in software and equipment, prompting the question: Why give away our hard-earned talent for free? I empathize with this sentiment, yet when we delve into the realms of marketing and promotion, where noise prevails, it becomes crucial to consider the ultimate goal and objective behind offering that free MP3 file.

Yes, you heard it right – I intentionally said "give." The underlying message is to recognize that the value of a mere file is determined by what you attribute to it. If you place a beat on that file, it's still a file, and the act of giving it away costs you nothing. The true value lies in the beat, capturing the attention of potential artists. This becomes particularly significant in a system like BuyBeats.com, where enticing users to sign up under your account and offering them a free beat creates an exchange.

What's the exchange, you might ask? It's the act of providing them with something they desire in return for their commitment to becoming a customer. This sets the stage for long-term value that extends beyond the initial free beat. As they explore your catalog with multiple beats, each play contributes to your stream revenue.

This isn't just about a one-time beat sale; it's about a continuous income stream, as these artists return to your platform.

Now, imagine a scenario where a customer, lured in by your free beat, explores thousands of beats on the platform. Even if they purchase someone else's beats, you still earn a 30% commission. It's time to adopt a more strategic approach to income generation. Instead of directing them to your personal website, where they might listen and leave, use social media wisely by encouraging them to hit the link in your bio on platforms like Instagram. This not only places them in your pipeline but opens avenues for a lifetime of income. It's about working smarter and wiser as producers in this new age, revolutionized by BuyBeats.com.

2 - SOUND SAMPLE KITS:

Lead Magnet: Offer a free sample kit containing unique and professionally crafted sounds.

Who needs a sound kit? Music producers can never have enough sounds, and if you can assemble a sound kit—even if it's just a snippet—it could serve as a valuable lead magnet, enticing producers to grab it for free. It's a straightforward process: compile a free sound kit on BuyBeats.com with the sounds you want to offer, as the platform allows you to upload up to two gigs of sounds in a free product offer.

To set this up, navigate to your dashboard's Customers tab, and simply add a beat offer. With that in place, all you need to do is broadcast the message that you have a free sound kit available. For instance, envision creating a video on your social media platform, be it TikTok or Instagram, where you showcase the sounds and inform producers that they can get them for free by hitting the link in your bio. Once they sign up, these sounds become their property, royalty-free.

Like the worm on the hook, some producers will seize the offer. Now, this producer is not just a casual browser; they're your customer on the BuyBeats.com platform. There are various outcomes that can unfold. They may remain inactive, which is a possibility, or they might decide to upgrade their account to become a premium user, driven by the messages they receive from the site highlighting the perks, including payment for beat placements. Now, you've successfully added a new producer to your customer network.

One fantastic aspect is that every time this producer's beats play on the platform, you earn a 30% commission—a continuous revenue stream for the lifetime of their beats on the platform. Consider the worm you've strategically placed on your hook, enticing music producers into your pipeline, creating numerous avenues for revenue generation on the platform.

3 - TUTORIAL VIDEOS:

Lead Magnet: Provide free tutorials on music production techniques in exchange for email sign-ups.

Now, this concept might be more accessible for some and challenging for others. If you're someone who enjoys creating videos, you can share techniques and insights into different Digital Audio Workstation (DAW) software or provide valuable tips. While a plethora of content is available on platforms like YouTube, adding your unique twist can make your teachings stand out. Instead of immediately opting to sell your knowledge, consider packaging it in a way that becomes enticing for your audience.

You might be thinking, "I don't want to give it away for free; I'll charge for it." However, putting a purchase price on it might not be as attractive. If you've discovered some quick ways or overcome obstacles that can benefit producers, spending an hour of your time teaching these insights can be valuable content. Offer this video tutorial in exchange for an email sign-up. Traditional marketing methods, such as utilizing an opt-in landing page, can prove beneficial in this scenario.

There are free resources available for setting up a webpage, and the concept is straightforward. Entice producers through social media or ads by saying, "Here's a new and effective technique for a specific task on this software. I want to show you how to do it, free. Click the link here on this page or in my bio, sign up, and on the next page, you'll receive video instructions on the topic." This approach is particularly effective if what you're offering holds substantial value.

By employing this strategy, you're building a list of engaged individuals whom you can regularly share valuable insights with. Having their email addresses allows you to engage with them through email, providing an opportunity to drop hints about your activities on the BuyBeats.com platform and gradually generate long-term income for yourself as you turn them into your customers.

4 - COLLABORATION OPPORTUNITIES:

Lead Magnet: Invite musicians to collaborate on a project and collect their contact information.

I briefly touched on collaboration in previous chapters, and I'd like to elaborate further on how you can establish a process to gain more leads by offering collaborations. It's a straightforward approach for both music producers and artists.

For artists, you can initiate a message indicating that you are actively seeking individuals who excel at creating hooks. Given that BuyBeats.com already has a split system for proceeds from beat sales, you can propose collaborations with rappers or artists, inviting them to work on hooks for your beats. This collaboration can result in having versions of your beats both with and without hooks. Artists who engage in this process become customers for you, contributing to your stream revenue as they explore your beats and others on the platform.

As for music producers, consider putting out a message expressing your willingness to collaborate with other producers for free. While some may charge for such collaborations, offering your services for free can lead to multiple producers collaborating with you. This not only enriches the collaborative experience but also contributes to your stream revenue, as the streams from their productions are uploaded to the platform.

It's a win-win situation. While charging for collaborations is an option, providing them for free can lead to a broader network of artists and producers to collaborate with, ultimately creating more opportunities for stream revenue. Holding out for payment might limit your potential gains, but by leveraging collaborations with various artists and producers, you open doors to a more extensive and potentially lucrative network.

5 - EXCLUSIVE WEBINAR OR WORKSHOP:

Lead Magnet: Free access to a live or recorded webinar on advanced music production techniques.

If you're a music producer with a significant following and others in the community admire and look up to you for your insights, you can leverage this interest by organizing a webinar or workshop.

In this session, you can share your successful strategies in music production, your approach to growing your Instagram following, and how you've achieved success in increasing your BuyBeats income.

By offering valuable information in this format, you create an opportunity for other producers to learn from your experiences. This can be a strategic way to build leads, as fellow producers may be keenly interested in understanding the specific steps you took to grow your Instagram following and enhance your income on BuyBeats.com.

Encourage users to sign up for the webinar or workshop, and the response could potentially yield a substantial number of leads. It's realistic to expect that out of, say, 100 sign-ups, 15 to 20 individuals might actively engage with your long-term income-generating plan. This engagement has the potential to translate into continuous income for years to come. Consider this approach as a targeted and effective way to share your knowledge while simultaneously building a community of engaged leads.

6 - LIVE Q&A SESSIONS:

Lead Magnet: Host live Q&A sessions where participants can submit questions in advance for exclusive access.

One powerful tool offered by Instagram and other platforms is the live feature, enabling you to connect directly with your audience. This presents various opportunities to capture leads. For instance, let's say you're planning an upcoming live session, perhaps discussing a topic with another producer. Before the live, encourage your audience to send in questions early.

By doing this, you create a channel for engagement, allowing individuals to either DM you or email their questions in advance.

This proactive approach enables you to initiate conversations with each person who has a question related to the upcoming topic.

If you decide to make this a recurring show, you can encourage people to DM you with questions they'd like to see covered in future episodes. This ongoing engagement not only provides valuable insights into what your audience is interested in but also opens opportunities to connect with your prospects individually, fostering a deeper relationship around the topics that resonate with them. Utilizing the live feature in this manner creates a dynamic and interactive space for lead generation.

7 - INTERACTIVE CHALLENGES:

Lead Magnet: Set up online challenges for producers to participate and share their entries for a chance to win prizes.

Social media provides an excellent platform for you to establish your presence in your specific area of focus. Whether you want to target recording artists or music producers, you can create engaging challenges tailored to each market. Here's how you can leverage this strategy:

Let's say you want to focus on music producers. You can organize challenges, such as a weekly trap contest, where producers can submit their trap beats for consideration. Once a week, you can compile a list of the top 10 submissions and promote them on your social media platforms.

This approach serves multiple purposes. Firstly, it positions you as an active and engaged figure in the producer community. Secondly, it provides value to producers by showcasing their work. Thirdly, and importantly, it continually connects you with potential customers—producers who may become long-term clients on the BuyBeats.com platform.

While this approach requires significant organization, and it may not be suitable for everyone, it offers a unique way to generate leads. By providing a service that brings value to your target market, you simultaneously create opportunities to grow your presence and network on the BuyBeats.com platform.

8 - THEMED PLAYLIST SUBMISSIONS:

Lead Magnet: Create themed playlists and invite artists to submit their tracks for consideration.

One outstanding feature of BuyBeats.com is its playlist functionality. Let's explore how you can use this feature as a lead generation tool to engage more producers and expand your network. This can be particularly effective when targeting specific genres or styles of beats.

Imagine you want to create a playlist featuring NBA YoungBoy type beats. You can post a graphic on your social media, announcing that you're compiling a playlist specifically for beats that NBA YoungBoy would jump on. In your call for producers to contribute, make it clear that they can be a part of this exclusive playlist by hitting the link in your bio and uploading their beats to the BuyBeats.com platform.

This process serves multiple purposes. Firstly, it turns these producers into your customers on the platform. Additionally, it invites them to audition for the playlist you're curating. This benefits the producer, yourself, and everyone involved in promoting that playlist.

Crucially, if this message reaches producers who may not yet be familiar with BuyBeats.com, offering them the opportunity to get on this playlist for free acts as a powerful incentive. By entering the system as your customer, you gain access to lifelong benefits, creating a mutually beneficial relationship for both you and the new producers entering the platform. This strategic use of playlists becomes a dynamic method for lead generation for your effort.

9 - MENTORSHIP PROGRAMS:

Lead Magnet: Offer a chance for aspiring producers to win mentorship sessions by signing up.

Becoming a mentor on BuyBeats.com is a fantastic idea, especially if you've achieved a level of expertise and success on the platform. Here's a simple strategy on how you could go about it:

Once you've reached the status of a successful hustler, many people may be interested in learning how you achieved that status, balancing your income against membership fees, and gaining insights into navigating the educational resources on the platform. You can leverage your expertise by putting out a message on your social media platforms. It could go something like this:

"Hey, do you want to learn how to make money like I do on one of the top beat production platforms? I've mastered the game, and I'm ready to share my secrets with you. DM me, and I'll show you how to earn money for your beat placements, build residual income, and thrive on this platform designed specifically for music producers and artists. Hit me up in the DM if you're interested!"

This message is designed to resonate with aspiring producers who are curious about alternative revenue streams and want to understand how to succeed on a specialized platform. Once you receive DMs expressing interest, you can initiate a conversation following the engagement techniques mentioned in the previous chapter. Once the person gives you permission to share information, you can seamlessly share your affiliate link, providing them with a direct pathway to join the platform through your mentorship. This approach allows you to mentor others while also potentially earning money through the affiliate program on BuyBeats.com.

10 - ARTIST SPOTLIGHTS:

Lead Magnet: Feature emerging artists on your platform and collect contacts for future collaborations.

Consider creating a hub that benefits artists instead of focusing solely on one Instagram account. Begin by establishing a dedicated Instagram page specifically designed to showcase new releases from recording artists. Utilize relevant hashtags like #unsignedartist to discover a diverse pool of artists who consistently share their content on Instagram.

Craft a message conveying your commitment to promoting new releases and independent music on this dedicated page. Reach out to artists with an offer to repost their content on this platform, promoting their work for free. While you don't necessarily need explicit permission to repost, this engagement adds value to the artists.

Through this act of promotion, you initiate introductions with artists, laying the groundwork for future engagements. As artists become familiar with your promotion hub, increased engagement provides opportunities to discuss their needs, potentially leading to collaborations or beat purchases.

Position yourself as a dedicated promoter of independent music, offering a valuable resource to artists and establishing connections that may evolve into potential customers or collaborators. This approach aligns with the overarching theme of building residual income by engaging with artists in a mutually beneficial manner.

11 - MAKE BEATS LIVES

Lead Magnet: Schedule a time once a week to go live making a beat then give the mp3 version away free.

Here's an engaging show idea for your artist community. Create anticipation by gradually building up suspense around the live creation of a beat. Once you complete the beat, announce that it's available for free download, but with a limited-time offer. For example, you can say, "The beat I just made will be exclusively available on my platform. Hit the link in the bio to grab it for free but act fast – it's only free for a week!"

This approach encourages artists to tune in to witness the live beat-making process and download the beat while it's still complimentary. To add an extra layer, set limitations on the free beats, making them available only as MP3 files with a restricted license. If artists wish to use the beat more extensively, they can upgrade and purchase the beat with a higher license for increased usability. This strategy not only generates excitement and engagement but also provides an opportunity for artists to invest in a higher-value product if they find the beat suitable for their needs.

12 - ENGAGE IN PRODUCER FORUMS & GROUPS

Lead Magnet: Take an hour or two from your weekly schedule to help others but also boast about your success on the BuyBeats.com platform.

Sharing your success on the BuyBeats.com platform is a positive way to engage with other producers in various online forums and communities. When discussions arise about the challenges producers face, you can tactfully mention that you no longer encounter those issues since joining BuyBeats.com. This sparks curiosity and prompts others to ask about the platform you're referring to.

In communities where self-promotion might be restricted, it's essential to navigate these guidelines thoughtfully. Instead of outright promoting BuyBeats.com, you can position yourself as a helpful resource. If someone expresses interest or asks which platform you're referring to, encourage them to send you a direct message for more information. This approach respects community guidelines while still creating opportunities for one-on-one conversations where you can share your positive experiences with BuyBeats.com and potentially lead them to your affiliate link.

Remember, the key is to offer value first, addressing concerns or challenges that other producers may be facing. By positioning yourself as a helpful and knowledgeable member of these communities, you naturally attract interest and inquiries about the platform that has brought you success.

13 - START A PODCAST OR YOUTUBE CHANNEL

Lead Magnet: Build a community around your music and production knowledge. Offer exclusive content or early access to new beats for subscribers.

Starting your own podcast or YouTube channel can indeed be highly beneficial, although it's important to acknowledge that building a successful platform requires time and effort. It's not as simple as appearing on camera and talking. However, a well-thought-out podcast can serve as a powerful lead magnet, drawing the interest of your target audience, especially if you cover specific topics that resonate with music producers.

The growth of a successful podcast or YouTube channel has the potential to generate valuable leads, contributing to the development of a significant residual income. Beyond the financial benefits, having a successful channel also brings other advantages. While the process may not be the easiest, when executed effectively, it can be one of the most rewarding endeavors in terms of audience engagement, community building, and establishing yourself as an authority in the field.

By consistently delivering high-quality content that appeals to your target audience, you create a platform that not only attracts leads but also fosters long-term relationships with your audience. This engagement can translate into various opportunities, from collaborations and partnerships to increased visibility and recognition within the music production community.

14 - RUN TARGETED ONLINE ADS:

Lead Magnet: Use platforms like Facebook Ads or Google Ads to reach specific demographics and interests with tailored messages.

Caution is indeed advised when using paid targeted online ads for lead generation, as it requires testing and careful crafting of advertising content. On platforms like Instagram and Facebook, utilizing the Boost Post feature can be effective, but it demands strategic planning.

Paid Targeted Online Ads: Approach with caution when utilizing paid targeted online ads for lead generation, as many producers have invested substantial amounts without seeing desired results. Testing and crafting compelling ad content are essential elements.

15 - BOOST POST FEATURE ON INSTAGRAM AND FACEBOOK:

The Boost Post feature on Instagram and Facebook can be a valuable tool when used judiciously. Posts, especially videos under a minute and 30 seconds or compelling still images, must resonate with your target audience—whether music producers or artists.

Strategic Spending: With careful spending, even a minimal budget like $10 can yield significant results. I have personally reached up to 4,000 accounts on Instagram and Facebook, generating 15 to 16 new users and 7 to 8 paid users. The return on investment, when factoring in residual income, can make this method well worth the effort.

Business Account Considerations: Note that, on Instagram, having a business account may be necessary to utilize the Boost Post feature effectively. Proceed with caution and consider the platform's guidelines and your specific audience when implementing this strategy.

16 - CREATE A PROFESSIONAL WEBSITE:

Lead Magnet: Showcase your work, testimonials, and services clearly and concisely. Include calls to action and easy-to-find contact information.

Creating your own website can be a highly effective strategy, especially when complemented with engaging content tailored for your target audience. While the necessity of a personal website may vary in an era dominated by social media, having an online presence can certainly add value.

Building Your Own Website: Establishing your own website can be a powerful move, provided you curate content that resonates with your target audience. While not indispensable in the age of social media dominance, having a dedicated online space can offer unique advantages.

Benefits of Having a Website: A website allows you to create distinct sections catering to different aspects of your brand. This could include various offers, informative content, and exclusive subscriptions. Some producers choose to have private subscription areas, offering exclusive content and additional perks, all operating under their brand umbrella.

Enhanced Outreach Efforts: Consider your website as an additional tool in your outreach efforts. It serves as a centralized hub where users can explore multiple facets of your brand, read informative content, and access various offers tailored to music producers and artists.

While not a mandatory component, having a website can enrich your overall strategy by providing a dedicated space for your brand and facilitating more targeted lead generation efforts.

17- YOUR SKILLS AND SERVICES

Lead Magnet: Many artists and music producers need specialized skills to enhance their projects.

Leveraging your skills in mixing and mastering can be a lucrative endeavor.

Promoting Mixing and Mastering Services: Utilize your well-honed skills in mixing and mastering by promoting these services on your Instagram account. You can either feature this on your existing account or create a separate one dedicated to showcasing your expertise.

Communicating Value: Craft a compelling message emphasizing the value you bring to artists and music producers by making their work sound exceptional through your mixing and mastering services. Clearly communicate that quality comes at a certain cost.

Strategic Promotion: While these services may not be offered for free, you can encourage potential clients to DM you for more information. In your response, provide details about your mixing and mastering packages and, at the same time, introduce them to additional services you offer.

Cross-Promotion with BuyBeats.com: Seize the opportunity to cross-promote by linking your mixing and mastering services with BuyBeats.com. For instance, if an artist approaches you for these services, you can recommend BuyBeats.com for acquiring more beats, emphasizing the potential to earn money through the platform.

Maximizing Marketing Efforts: Integrate your marketing efforts, turning potential clients for mixing and mastering into long-term prospects on BuyBeats.com. This allows you to generate lifetime residuals from their engagement with various services, creating a mutually beneficial relationship.

18 - CREATE YOUR OWN BLOG:

Lead Magnet: Blog posts, or articles, are published regularly and can appear in social feeds and be emailed to subscribers.

Some may not distinguish between websites and blogs. A website typically has static pages, infrequently updated, focusing on the owner's content. In contrast, a blog is dynamic, involving regular posting of articles on specific topics.

Imagine having a blog on music production tips, releasing articles on equipment used in studios, techniques, software tricks, and more. With a consistent posting schedule, each blog post, ranging from 500 to 1,000 words, becomes a valuable resource. The goal is to draw an audience over time, converting them into potential leads for other projects and offers.

Over a year, a well-maintained blog can amass a loyal following. This audience eagerly returns for the insightful tips you offer. Meanwhile, strategically placed banners within the blog can direct them to other offers, such as BuyBeats.com. Encouraging visitors to subscribe to your newsletter ensures they receive updates and additional promotions directly to their inbox.

Inside the blog posts, strategically position banners and information about your various offerings. While staying loyal to the blog's topic, subtly introduce other relevant offers alongside the articles. This indirect approach maintains the integrity of the content while subtly promoting your additional services.

For those interested, the bonus AI chapter at the end of this book discusses tools that can facilitate blog management, making it easier to maintain and optimize your lead generation system.

19 - OFFER ARTIST DEVELOPMENT SERVICES:

Lead Magnet: You can offer artists development services that will put you in front of your target audience.

If you have skills in artist development and can assist artists in structuring their songs and creating EPs or LPs, it's an opportunity to generate leads. While you don't have to accept every artist into your program, marketing and attracting artists can introduce them to the offerings at BuyBeats.com. If you can't help a particular artist, you can still guide them towards other producers available on the platform. Encourage them to sign up for free using your link, creating a win-win situation where you benefit from their activity as an artist on BuyBeats.com.

20 - HOST PRODUCER MASTERMIND GROUPS:

Lead Magnet: Utilize online platforms like Clubhouse or Zoom to create mastermind groups for producers to share strategies, receive feedback, and hold each other accountable. Offer paid membership with lead capture for access.

Platforms like Clubhouse, Zoom, and other audio chat features offer an opportunity to establish Mastermind groups with fellow producers. This provides a space to share strategies, offer feedback, and explore collaborative efforts to collectively grow in the field of music production. Whether a paid or free opportunity, it has the potential to attract other producers, whom you can introduce to the opportunities on BuyBeats.com. Building momentum for such a venture requires time and dedication but can be incredibly rewarding.

21 – HOST PRODUCER FEEDBACK LIVE STREAMS:

Lead Magnet: Conduct live feedback sessions where producers submit tracks and receive suggestions.

Producers are often seeking validation, feedback, and ways to improve their craft. Fortunately, there are numerous outlets available, and you can become one for producers. They can DM you and submit tracks for broadcast, inviting other producers to chime in with feedback and suggestions for improvement. A great example of this is Jones on the Beat, who operates within the BuyBeats.com community, focusing on promoting producers on the platform and curating lists for everyone to participate in the money-making incentives offered by BuyBeats.com. While you don't have to replicate Jones on the Beat's approach exactly, there are various ways you can attract producers and build a community around what

BuyBeats.com is providing for music producers. For more information, visit @beatpromoters on Instagram.

22- BONUS - EBOOK OR GUIDE ON MUSIC PRODUCTION:

Lead Magnet: A downloadable eBook or guide sharing insights, tips, and tricks for music producers.

Another effective way to attract your prospects is by offering helpful eBooks that they can download. It doesn't take much time to put together an eBook, especially with the advanced technology we have, including AI (artificial intelligence). In the paperback version of this book, there's an entire chapter dedicated to guiding you on how to create an eBook quickly. A free eBook sharing insights, tips, tricks, and more is an excellent strategy to build up your contact list. This contact list will consist of individuals who are genuinely interested in the information you provide and are likely to opt into your offers.

In this book, "Residual Income for Music Producers," designed for members of BuyBeats.com, a valuable resource is available as soon as individuals sign up in the bonus office section. Even if you don't have your own eBook to promote, you can share a chapter from this book in a video. Explain how the techniques discussed in the book are generating income for you. Invite producers to hit the link in the bio to instantly download their free copy. Whether it's this book or other valuable information you want to compile into an eBook, the approach remains just as effective.

Remember, these 21 lead generation strategies are just starting points. Don't be afraid to get creative and combine these ideas to develop your own unique and impactful lead generation strategies for your music production business. The key is to provide genuine value and engage with your audience to build a strong and loyal community.

Chapter 13

Case Study: $4,000 in Residual Income Earned in 3 Months!

I have witnessed BuyBeats.com evolve from its humble beginnings with Sensei Jay and myself to become a thriving platform hosting thousands of talented producers today. Throughout this incredible journey, I've seen a multitude of producers come and go, some grappling to grasp the platform's concept, while others have seized the opportunity, building substantial residual income streams in addition to selling their beats. In this chapter, I aim to spotlight the stories of four exceptional music producers who not only comprehended the program but are excelling at generating residual income, employing diverse strategies and techniques to expand their networks.

One of these remarkable producers is DJ Luigi, introduced to the platform through Monique Winning. DJ Luigi had been an active member for approximately six months, steadily ascending to the esteemed "hustler" status within a remarkably short period. He approached the program with unwavering commitment and a profound understanding, wholeheartedly dedicated to cultivating his residual income. DJ Luigi demonstrated his commitment by uploading a staggering 500 plus beats to BuyBeats.com, showcasing his dedication to the platform's success from the very beginning.

Monique Winning, the producer who extended the invitation to DJ Luigi, initially captivated my attention through a ProducerGrind interview on YouTube. During this interview, Monique elaborated on her impressive achievements and triumphs in the music production industry. Monique's distinction as a certified RIAA music producer, signifying her involvement in projects that achieved gold status (500,000 copies sold), was truly impressive. Intrigued by her accomplishments, I decided to reach out to her and introduce BuyBeats.com. While she liked the concept, she did not immediately dive in.

At that time, BuyBeats.com was still emerging, prompting Monique to adopt a cautious approach, allowing the platform to establish itself and prove its merit. As we continued refining the platform's concept and enhancing its features, Monique eventually took to Instagram, where she boasted an impressive following of 25,000 at the time. Her endorsement significantly bolstered the platform's exposure and momentum, with her positive response serving as a valuable validation of BuyBeats.com. Consequently, she continues to promote and repost about the platform from time to time.

The third producer we're spotlighting here is ValentinBeatz, who has been making significant strides on the platform. ValentinBeatz introduction to BuyBeats.com came through DJ Luigi's referral. After joining the platform, ValentinBeatz diligently studied its nuances, quickly recognizing its potential for growth. Remarkably, in just over four months, he accrued over $1,300 in residual income and an additional $500 from beat sales and beat plays. ValentinBeatz diligently implemented numerous strategies outlined in this book, consistently sharing his earnings on Instagram and extending invitations to fellow producers interested in learning about multiple income streams.

Now, let's turn our attention to another remarkable producer, BeatsByCasual, introduced to the platform by ValentinBeatz. BeatsByCasual is a producer who possesses a profound understanding of the marketing aspects within the music industry. With an impressive following of approximately 35,000 Instagram followers, he has effectively showcased his skills in building a robust online presence.

BeatsByCasual has harnessed every facet of the platform, ingeniously transforming them into lucrative income sources. Astonishingly, within just four months of joining the platform, he has achieved an impressive total sales count of $2,700. This remarkable sum encompasses $398 generated from beat sales and an astounding $2,300 in subscription revenue. This exemplifies the type of partnership with BuyBeats.com that enables individuals to maximize the profit-sharing system. BeatsByCasual success serves as a shining testament to how a producer can translate actions that might be undertaken freely on other platforms into a consistent monthly income, one that continually ascends to greater heights with each passing month.

My primary objective here is to cast a spotlight on these exceptional producers and shed light on the tactics and strategies they have employed to fuel their growth on BuyBeats.com. Following is an in-depth case study that delves into their journeys and accomplishments as observed by me, providing valuable insights into their successful endeavors on the platform.

PRODUCER MONIQUE WINNING

The first producer I'd like to spotlight is Monique Winning. Monique has not only grown her Instagram account to an impressive 25,000 plus followers but also manages another account called " @MogulProducers." When you visit her page, it's evident that she's a dedicated hustler. While she occasionally shares personal aspects of her life, her main focus is on engaging with her audience and promoting her beat-making ventures and various products. One notable trait of Monique is her consistent introduction of new concepts, ideas, production software and platforms to her followers. Her entrepreneurial spirit shines through, and it's easy to see why she achieves success.

One day, Monique posted about collaborating, which aligned perfectly with our previous conversations. Seizing the opportunity, we discussed some business matters, and she created a concise video, lasting no more than a minute, highlighting the unique features of BuyBeats.com. In this video, she covered aspects about the paid Beat Plays and the Beat Request system, emphasizing the unique qualities of the platform. The key move that elevated this collaboration was Monique's call to action at the end of the video. She directed both artists and music producers to click on the link in her bio. Upon visiting her bio, I found a link management system with about ten links. The first link was tailored for music producers to click, while the second was for recording artists to click. When that video went live, sign-ups started pouring onto the platform, establishing Monique as one of BuyBeats.com's top referrers.

Following this successful collaboration, Monique continued to share information about the platform with her audience. One particularly effective post highlighted five artists simultaneously submitting Beat requests. Monique's strategic approach was evident when multiple producers signed up under her link. She posted a message inviting producers who were tired of searching for artists to join the platform, emphasizing that artists were actively looking for producers. By outlining specific criteria for beat requests and artists sharing their budgets, she attracted approximately an additional 50 producers to BuyBeats.com. Consequently, Monique now earns stream income from all those producers' beat play revenue and has allowed her to earn shared commissions from their subscriptions.

While it may seem that Monique's success is solely due to her substantial following of 25,000 followers, it's essential to remember that it's not just about the number of followers but the quality of engagement with your audience. Even with a smaller follower count, if you consistently provide value and seize opportunities, you can achieve remarkable results. Building a genuine connection with your audience and presenting valuable opportunities when they arise is the key to success.

PRODUCER DJ LUIGI

As mentioned earlier, DJ Luigi joined the platform and has been diligently grinding since. One of his initial moves was creating a presentation video where he effectively showcased BuyBeats.com's unique features. He promptly shared this video in his Instagram story, and anyone who viewed it had access to his invite link to the platform. Instead of merely mentioning BuyBeats.com, he strategically included his invite link within the story.

DJ Luigi's commitment to building a robust profile was evident in his uploading of over 500 beats. This action signified his dedication to the platform. Additionally, those 500+ beats yielded regular payouts from beat play income. This smart move ensured that his beats were not dormant on some platform's hard drive, generating no income. DJ Luigi comprehended this crucial point and acted accordingly.

On Instagram, DJ Luigi was actively engaged. He frequently liked and commented on people's posts, whether on platforms like Producer Grind or major artist profiles. His light green icon seemed to appear everywhere, signifying his active presence within the music production community. His efforts did not go unnoticed, and somehow, he caught the attention of ValentinBeatz.

ValentinBeatz, a significant player on the BuyBeats.com platform, ended up signing up under DJ Luigi's invite link. This connection brought substantial benefits to DJ Luigi. Due to DJ Luigi's invitation, he now receives 10% of all the subscription fees generated by ValentinBeatz on the platform. Not only that, but he also gets 30% of the stream revenue from all of ValentinBeatz' tracks that are played by recording artists.

Throughout this book, I've stressed that BuyBeats.com stands out by rewarding its producers. While other platforms charge membership fees ranging from $15 to $20 per month and keep the entire amount, BuyBeats.com compensates its producers based on their marketing efforts and network growth. DJ Luigi's position highlights the rewarding nature of this system.

BuyBeats.com, at the time of writing this book, is not even two years old, but it holds great promise for everyone who joins at this early stage. DJ Luigi has achieved the status of a hustler and now enjoys a steadily increasing monthly income. This growth trajectory is a testament to the opportunities BuyBeats.com offers to those who seize them.

PRODUCER VALENTINBEATZ

ValentinBeatz, who was introduced to the platform by DJ Luigi, initially took his time to thoroughly review BuyBeats.com. However, once he grasped the program's potential, he jumped in with full throttle. He recognized that this platform offered producers more than any other existing platform, providing an opportunity for them to maximize their earnings. With honesty and authenticity, he encouraged fellow producers to capitalize on this opportunity.

ValentinBeatz' first posts were aligned with this sentiment, emphasizing the unique benefits of BuyBeats.com. After each post, he consistently urged producers to reach out to him via direct messages (DMs) to learn more. This approach resulted in an overwhelming number of producers flooding his DMs, eager to gain insights into this promising opportunity.

One notable aspect of ValentinBeatz strategy was his willingness to go live and discuss the platform with groups of producers. During these live sessions, he passionately explained how BuyBeats.com represented the next big thing in the industry. His conviction was well-founded, as BuyBeats.com indeed introduced an innovative approach unmatched by other platforms. In almost every post, he continued to praise the platform and encouraged fellow producers to join the movement.

VALENTINBEATZ EARNED $2,006.14
INCOME IN JUST 4 MONTHS ON BUYBEATS!

In just over three months on the platform, ValentinBeatz had already earned over $1,500. At the time of writing this book, he had surpassed the $2,000 mark, showcasing tremendous potential. It wouldn't be surprising if, in the next six to seven months, he was consistently earning $4,000 or more each month on the platform.

ValentinBeatz' Instagram profile serves as a valuable resource for those looking to learn from his success. With over 50,000 followers, he frequently shares insights about the platform, providing valuable guidance to other producers. He engages his audience by posing thought-provoking questions, showcasing his latest and hottest beats, and encouraging artists to rate his productions on a scale of 1 to 10. When artists express interest, he promptly sends them a link via DM.

For a more detailed overview of ValentinBeatz journey on the platform, you can visit our blog, where you'll find a comprehensive video highlighting his achievements. As an affiliate, you can share this link with potential producers, allowing them to witness what can be achieved in a relatively short period.

You can share this link. Switch "Your-Username" in link with your BuyBeats.com username.

Your Promo Link
https://buybeats.com/Your-Username/freetraining

PRODUCER BEATSBYCASUAL

Producer BeatsByCasual is an actively engaged member of our platform. A glance at his posts reveals a diverse range of content. He not only shares his thoughts and concerns regarding the challenges faced by producers but also takes a stand against any injustices within the community. BeatsByCasual boasts a highly engaged following, and every post he shares resonates deeply with his audience. What sets him apart is his willingness to share his emotions and personal experiences, giving his followers a glimpse of the human side behind the producer.

If you visit his profile at BeatsByCasual, you'll witness firsthand the authenticity and engagement he brings to our platform.

BeatsByCasual maintains a strong presence and actively interacts with his followers, offering them unwavering support.

When ValentinBeatz introduced BeatsByCasual to BuyBeats.com, it marked the beginning of an exciting journey. BeatsByCasual initiated a conversation with me to understand the opportunity better, displaying an openness to explore new horizons. Once he comprehended the platform's vision, he embraced it wholeheartedly. BeatsByCasual stands out as a genuinely nice guy, offering valuable insights and wisdom from his unique perspective.

Upon grasping the platform's potential, he wasted no time in sharing the BuyBeats.com opportunity with his audience. However, BeatsByCasual didn't stop at mere promotion; he extended a helping hand by providing insights into the platform's functionalities, illustrating how it surpasses other industry alternatives. Within a week or two, he began sharing his initial results, effectively showcasing the platform's potential for success.

One intriguing tactic BeatsByCasual employs is posting content and occasionally removing it after about 12 hours or sooner. While the exact reason for this strategy remains unclear, it effectively keeps his audience engaged and might even align with Instagram's algorithm. In addition to sharing his progress,

BeatsByCasual occasionally posts snippets of beats he's working on, engaging both artists and fellow producers on his Instagram page.

While BeatsByCasual bio doesn't always feature a link or the techniques mentioned earlier, he actively responds to comments and readily invites interested individuals to reach out via DM. The power of the DMs lies in the fact that they serve as a conduit for sharing unique referral links, ensuring credit for those who sign up.

Although I can't provide concrete evidence, I suspect that BeatsByCasual leverages other platforms to drive traffic to his BuyBeats.com offer. This tactic aligns with his commitment to maximizing his success on the platform.

Towards the end of 2023, BeatsByCasual expressed his gratitude for discovering BuyBeats.com. He reflected on the challenges he faced during the year and highlighted BuyBeats.com as one of the best things to happen to him in 2023. While his posts may shift around on his profile, you may still come across this heartfelt message.

BEATSBYCASUAL EARNED $2,735.16 INCOME IN JUST 4 MONTHS ON BUYBEATS!

BeatsByCasual commitment to helping his followers and active engagement in various communities is evident. His impressive earnings of $2,735 in just four months on BuyBeats.com underscore the platform's potential, even in its early stages. Startups typically require several years to gain momentum, but with the talent and dedication displayed by producers like BeatsByCasual, BuyBeats.com is well on its way to success. These producers have demonstrated that with dedication and a great platform like BuyBeats.com, you can build a sustainable income stream, even when beat sales aren't the primary focus. The system is here, waiting for you to fully capitalize on its potential and take your music production journey to the next level.

Phase 3

Welcome to Phase 3, where we shift from the practical steps of using BuyBeats.com to a deeper, more personal mentorship. Think of this phase as a one-on-one session where I share a lot I've learned about wealth building and mindset shaping. It's like we're sitting together in a quiet, comfortable space, ready to dive into the heart of what it takes to succeed.

In our journey together so far, you've learned how to leverage the platform and grow your client base. Now, I want to take you a step further. I'm going to share my personal experiences, the teachings from my mentors, and the key lessons that have profoundly shaped my approach to success in the music industry.

This isn't just about sharing stories; it's about imparting wisdom that can fundamentally change how you view your career and life. I'll be open and honest about my challenges, my triumphs, and the mindset shifts that have been crucial in my journey.

So, let's get started on this final phase. I'm here to guide you, inspire you, and equip you with the tools to think, produce, and succeed like never before. It's time to shape your mindset for extraordinary achievements in music production and beyond.

Chapter 14

My First Millionaire Mentor's Wisdom: Personal Insights for Success

From my earliest memories, I've always been entrepreneurial. At just 12 years old, instead of riding bikes or playing with GI Joes like other kids in my neighborhood, I was busy dreaming up business plans. I remember thinking, "What if I could get a million people to give me just $1? That would make me a millionaire, right?" These weren't just idle daydreams; they were my first steps towards financial freedom.

During those early years, I dabbled in various entrepreneurial activities. I shoveled snow, delivered newspapers, raked leaves, and even sold autographs, which is a story in itself. These experiences were crucial in developing the entrepreneurial mindset that would define my future, though I didn't fully grasp it at the time.

It wasn't until I was 18 or 19, running my first barbershop, that I truly understood what being an entrepreneur meant. I wasn't academically inclined – I barely scraped through high school – so the term 'entrepreneur' was foreign to me. If someone had asked if I was a businessman, I would've confidently said yes. But when a customer introduced me to the term entrepreneurship at 19, it was the first time I ever heard of the word.

I began cutting hair at 14, quickly becoming proficient and popular in my neighborhood. By 15, I was working in a barbershop, and by 19, I owned one. Making about $1500 a week, I felt like I'd made it big. However, my understanding of success and wealth was about to change dramatically.

My landlord, a humble Korean man named David, whom I initially mistook for a maintenance worker due to his modest appearance, was the catalyst for this change. Our conversations started with small talk about my flashy clothes and abundance of sneakers. His questions to me would be, "Why are you putting all your money in those things." He was always changing my perspective when it came to spending money. One day, he shared a piece of wisdom that altered my perspective on wealth. He pointed out that while I worked every day to earn money, he only needed to show up once a month to collect rent. He explained that from the 13-store building, he collected $40,000 a month rent from two restaurants, a salon, my barbershop and other businesses. This was my first lesson on assets building wealth and not you personally.

David's insight was a pivotal moment in my life. It taught me the importance of investing in assets that generate income, a concept that I had been unmindful to until then. He opened my eyes to the idea that one could build wealth by being part of a system that works for you, rather than working for it.

Sharing this story is not just about recounting my journey, but also about offering you a new perspective on wealth and success. It's about understanding the value of assets and passive income. While I wasn't ready to buy a building at 19, I made it a life goal to invest in assets that would generate passive income.

WHAT SHOULD I DO WITH THIS MONEY!

Running my barbershop, I would occasionally catch up with David. These conversations, especially as a 19 and 20-year-old, were incredibly valuable. A few years into knowing David, I found myself with about $100,000 from the sale of a home. Curious about what my mentor would suggest, I made a special trip to seek his advice. "Hey David, I've got this lump sum of money; what do you think I should do with it?" His response was thought-provoking. "I can't tell you exactly what to do, but whatever you do, you must leverage it." I was puzzled. "What does he mean by leverage?" This question marked the beginning of another significant life lesson, a key to understanding how millionaires are made. Leverage, I learned, is the secret ingredient in all wealth-building.

Eager for clarity, I pressed David further. "What exactly is leverage? How should I use it?" He explained, "You have to invest the money in a system, product, or service that will continuously generate revenue for you. You can't just be the system, the product, or the service." He went on to give me even more details. This conversation changed everything. It deepened my understanding and opened my eyes to a new way of thinking.

Back in my barbershop, I began to see things differently. Looking at a container of powder on the table, I realized, "Whoever makes this powder is doing better than me. This powder isn't just in my shop; it's in a million other shops. That's leverage!" Suddenly, everything in the shop took on a new meaning. The clippers I used daily were not just tools for my trade, but symbols of duplicatable success. "The manufacturer of these clippers made millions of them, selling each for $50, $60, or $100 to millions of barbers worldwide. His family became extremely wealthy, while I show up every day to make money using their product." This realization was a pivotal moment in the development of my wealth mindset.

This shift in perspective led me to an important conclusion: "I can't just work on the system; I need to have the system working for me. I can't just use the product; I need to benefit from each sale of the product." This principle of leverage is at the heart of BuyBeats.com for every user rather than an artist or music producer. As a music producer, you can still offer your beats for sale on BuyBeats.com and elsewhere. However, the real concept behind BuyBeats.com, often overlooked, is the opportunity for you to leverage your time and effort to build a steady stream of residual and passive income following the system.

Many music producers who overlook the concept behind BuyBeats.com miss the essence of what it truly offers. This is why I feel compelled to share the wisdom imparted to me at the age 19 from David. A significant monthly cash flow can only be achieved by understanding how assets should work for you, not just for others.

These lessons were my first insights from David, my millionaire mentor. Now, I want to get into it a bit deeper and share more from the wisdom I've gained from my other millionaire mentors.

David Gong January 2024

Logical Points for Chapter 15 - My First Millionaire Mentor:

Entrepreneurial Beginnings and the Power of Observation:
The author's early entrepreneurial activities and keen observations set the stage for a lifelong journey in business. This chapter highlights the importance of nurturing an entrepreneurial spirit from a young age and the impact of being observant about one's surroundings. Why limit oneself to conventional childhood activities when early entrepreneurial experiences can pave the way for future success?

Discovering the Essence of Entrepreneurship:
The realization and self-identification as an entrepreneur, catalyzed by interactions in the barbershop, signify a pivotal moment in the author's life. This point underscores the importance of self-awareness and external influences in understanding one's true potential and professional calling. Why wait for external validation when self-discovery can lead to profound career revelations?

Lessons in Leverage from a Millionaire Mentor:
The author's mentorship with David, the landlord, provides invaluable insights into the concept of leverage and passive income. This part of the chapter illustrates how mentorship can unlock new perspectives and understanding of wealth creation. Why rely solely on personal experiences when mentorship can

offer a shortcut to wisdom and success?

A Shift in Wealth Mindset:
The transformation of the author's mindset from a labor-based income approach to a focus on generating passive income through assets is a key takeaway. This shift in perspective is crucial for anyone looking to move beyond active income to building long-term wealth. Why continue in the cycle of active income when a shift in mindset can open doors to wealth accumulation?

The Impact of Real-World Examples on Business Acumen:
Observing everyday items like barber shop powder and clippers, and understanding their role in a larger economic system, demonstrates practical business acumen. This point emphasizes the value of learning from real-world examples to gain practical business insights. Why overlook everyday items when they can be sources of profound business lessons?

Chapter 15

How I Turned $8 into Millions

The title "How I Turned $8 into Millions" might raise some eyebrows, possibly evoking skepticism from certain readers. If this includes you, I hope to shift your perspective. For those with an open mind, the concepts I'm about to share could be pivotal in developing, building, or achieving a level of success. An open mind is crucial in this journey.

I vividly remember a time in a Clubhouse room, a popular app at the time. I was speaking to a crowd of about 200 people. I began to share my belief that it doesn't necessarily take money to make money. This idea immediately faced resistance. Some attendees quickly jumped to conclusions, criticizing my point of view, and even suggesting that I be removed from the conversation. However, I wasn't offended. Their reactions simply indicated a difference in mindset and a lack of exposure to the ideas I had come to understand. The moderator, curious, encouraged me to elaborate, wanting to know how I managed to turn a mere $8 into millions.

Before I delve into the specifics of my $8 journey, it's important to understand the mindset that made this possible. When I was 22, sitting in my barbershop, I had a moment of realization. I needed something more – knowledge that could take me further. This led me to Barnes and Noble, not knowing exactly what I was looking for but knowing I needed something enlightening. There, in Queens, right behind Queens Boulevard at 71st and Continental (a familiar spot to locals), I found my answer in the business section.

The book that caught my eye was "Zero Down Real Estate Deals" by Tyler G Hicks. Something about it piqued my interest. As I flipped through the pages, I knew I had to have it. It wasn't just about the content; it was how the content was presented – different ways of explaining things that I hadn't considered before. I decided to add this book to my arsenal. The next day, between haircuts and in moments of downtime, I began to absorb the book.

The concepts and principles in that book were timeless. The more I read, the more enthused I became. It was like discovering a treasure trove of knowledge that I never knew existed. What surprised me the most, however, was something I found at the end of the book. The author had included his phone number, inviting readers to call him for assistance. This was unprecedented in my experience – an author, reachable and willing to offer help beyond his written words.

Intrigued and somewhat skeptical, I decided to call the number. The voice that answered confirmed, "This is Tyler Hicks." I was taken aback, speaking directly to the author whose book I was holding in my hands. We discussed the book briefly before the conversation took a more personal turn. Tyler, a prolific author and self-help guru, had published over 130 books and publications and was a well-known figure in the self-help publishing world. This was information I would learn more about later. But at that moment, I was just amazed to be talking to him.

Our conversation led to an opportunity I couldn't pass up. I expressed interest in one of his kits, and Tyler invited me to his home to pick it up. Driving to Long Island, I was filled with a mix of excitement and curiosity. When I arrived at his house, a beautiful mansion set in a picturesque neighborhood, I was in awe. The experience of buying a book and then standing at the author's house was surreal. It was a moment that defied the norms of my world, where such openness and hospitality were rare.

Sitting on Tyler's porch, the reality of where I was and who I was with started to sink in. This was a man who had achieved the kind of success many only dream of. The kit I purchased from him for $99 was the beginning of a mentorship and a relationship that would influence my understanding of business and wealth building. Over time, I invested a significant amount in learning from Tyler, but it was more than just the financial transactions. It was the opportunity to glean wisdom from our conversations, to be in the presence of someone who had mastered the art of building wealth from minimal resources.

Tyler's teaching centered around the concept of building significant ventures with little to no initial investment. This was not just theoretical knowledge but practical, actionable insights. It was about understanding the power of negotiation, leveraging other people's resources, and recognizing opportunities that others might overlook. This philosophy became a cornerstone of my approach to business and life.

Applying Tyler's teachings to my ventures proved transformative. The most notable example was the creation of rocbattle.com. Starting with an $8 investment in a domain name, this project required capabilities beyond my skill set. However, applying the principles I had learned from Tyler, I negotiated with a team of programmers. Instead of paying a large sum upfront, we agreed on a profit-sharing arrangement. This was a practical application of Tyler's strategy, showcasing the importance of resourcefulness and strategic partnerships.

Since then, I've replicated this approach in various ventures, each reinforcing the idea that substantial achievements are possible with limited resources. These experiences have underscored the importance of an open-minded approach to business and the power of seizing even the smallest opportunities.

Reflecting on my journey with Tyler G. Hicks, it's clear that his influence extended beyond business strategies. He taught me life lessons about innovation, and the power of thinking differently. His philosophy—that you don't need money to make money, but rather ideas, concepts, and smart processing—has been a guiding force in my journey from minimal investment to significant wealth.

In closing this chapter, I pay homage to Tyler G. Hicks, who passed away in March 2020. His teachings and the impact he had on my life and career continue to resonate with me. He showed me that the journey from a small investment to substantial wealth is not just a financial endeavor; it's a journey of the mind, embracing new ideas and approaches. Thank you, Tyler Hicks, for that invaluable lesson.

Logical Point for "How I Turned $8 into Millions":

The Unconventional Path to Wealth:
The author's journey from making a skeptical phone call to a renowned author to visiting his mansion in Long Island exemplifies an unconventional but effective path to wealth. It's a vivid illustration that success often lies beyond traditional methods and in the willingness to take risks and embrace unique opportunities. Why follow the beaten path when this story illuminates a less traveled road to financial success?

Leveraging Minimal Resources for Maximum Impact:
This narrative showcases the author's mastery in transforming a minimal $8 investment into a lucrative business venture. It emphasizes the power of strategic negotiation and resourcefulness, proving that significant achievements don't always require substantial capital. Why be constrained by limited resources when this chapter demonstrates how to turn small investments into great successes?

The Importance of Mentorship and Continuous Learning:
The author's relationship with Tyler Hicks highlights the impact of mentorship and the continuous pursuit of knowledge. It shows that success is also about the wisdom gleaned from others and the application of learned principles. Why journey alone when mentorship can be a guiding light towards success?

Turning Challenges into Opportunities:
The development of rocbattle.com, despite initial technical limitations, illustrates how perceived challenges can be transformed into opportunities. It's a testament to the author's ability to see beyond obstacles and find innovative solutions. Why view challenges as roadblocks when they can be steppingstones to success?

The Power of Strategic Partnerships:
The chapter emphasizes the significance of strategic partnerships and collaborations in business growth. The negotiation with programmers for rockbattle.com serves as a prime example of mutual benefit through smart alliances. Why limit potential by going solo when strategic partnerships can amplify success?

A Mindset for Innovative Entrepreneurship:
This story is not just about financial gains; it's about cultivating a mindset for innovative entrepreneurship. It's a journey that challenges conventional thinking and showcases the power of creativity and strategic planning in business. Why settle for traditional methods when an innovative mindset can open doors to unprecedented success?

Chapter 16

Maximizing Your Assets: The Blueprint for Obtaining Wealth

Delve into the blueprint for obtaining wealth by maximizing your assets. Discover strategies that can accelerate your income and ensure financial stability.

EMOTIONAL ATTACHMENT AND BUSINESS PERSPECTIVE IN MUSIC PRODUCTION

Many music producers don't consciously think about their real assets. Before delving into this lesson, I need to address a common issue I've observed among many in the music production business. Often, the love for one's own creations overshadows the business aspects that should be prioritized. Sometimes, the emotions invested in the creative process can cloud judgment regarding the business moves you should be making. Let's clarify this point, as it can make or break your music career.

THE ANALOGY OF REAL ESTATE AND MUSIC ASSETS

Let me share an analogy that was told to me long ago, which you might find relatable as a real estate investor. My friends in real estate, adhering to some conventional wisdom, advised that when you buy your first rental property, you should not fall in love with it. Many investors, starting from humble beginnings, beautify their new property and then, rather than renting it out as planned, move into it themselves. They let their emotions take over, abandoning the logic of building their portfolio for a few more years. So, why do I tell this story to you, a music producer? What do real estate or emotions have to do with you? At the core, what I'm getting at is this: real estate is an asset. Similarly, the music you produce and the skills you possess are assets because they can generate income through various mediums. We'll delve deeper into this later, so you can understand which mediums are most effective for wealth generation. But what I want to emphasize in this chapter is that many producers struggle to advance because they are too emotionally attached to their assets.

THE PITFALL OF EMOTIONAL ATTACHMENT TO CREATIONS

Over the years, I've talked to numerous producers and offered concepts on how they could make more money or diversify their skills and creations into other mediums. Often, I encounter resistance because they can't see beyond their attachment to their beats. Let me break it down further. A producer might create a hundred beats, but because they can't bear the thought of their favorite rapper, or even a decent one, not rapping on their beat, they hold onto it closely. They don't release it from their hard drive. These are assets that you're hoarding due to emotional attachment.

THE RULE OF DETACHMENT AND PRODUCTIVITY

Here's a crucial rule: Do not get attached to your creations. The more you release your creations, the more you'll realize that you're capable of producing even better work. If you believe that you can't create a beat as good as the one you're holding onto, you hinder the flow of your creative juices. You need the mindset that once a beat is released into the market, it's there to work for you, to be leveraged as much as possible, and you shouldn't worry about it any further. The quickest path to downfall and not making money in music production is to care too much.

I know this may go against what some believe. You might be waiting for a specific artist to jump on your track or for a certain buyer to come along. However, that wait could last forever. So, do you want to stop building something for yourself because you're clinging to a dream that might never materialize? Consider this: there are hundreds of thousands of producers with the same dream. How many opportunities are there for all these producers at once? Think about how you can maximize your own assets and start building to produce the level of income you desire right now with what you have.

YOU ARE AN ASSET MAKING MACHINE

Now that I've addressed the emotional aspect, let's focus on recognizing your potential as an asset-making machine. If you're a producer capable of whipping up beats in a half day or even two, or if you can churn out at least 15 halfway decent beats a month, you're already on the right track. Remember, even halfway decent beats have a market. You're capable of pushing assets into the marketplace, and it's crucial to detach emotionally from each creation.

With the unique setup of BuyBeats.com, we've flipped the script. There are artists willing to pay for your beats, and there are those who want freebies. But now, with our new system, your asset works either way. For artists seeking free beats, give it to them with a catch: have them sign up, listen to a certain number of tracks, and then they can choose a free beat from a designated section. This way, you're strategically using beats to build a listener base and potential customers while still getting paid. Imagine having four or five hundred assets in place. Now, it's about leveraging what the system provides to generate the income you need.

ADAPTING TO MARKET DYNAMICS AND INNOVATIVE ASSET MANAGEMENT

It's vital to understand and adapt to the current market dynamics. The way beats are sold has evolved, and holding onto outdated models or getting frustrated with these changes won't help. Instead, it's about figuring out how your assets can work for you in new ways. It's about being innovative and flexible in your approach to asset management and sales.

LONG-TERM STRATEGY FOR ASSET UTILIZATION

Now, as we discuss your assets, I often see producers selling their beats for exclusive fees of just $100, $200, or $300. I ask myself, why? That asset has the potential, over time, to generate much more than $100. Plus, with non-exclusive licensing, you retain ownership. You don't have to give it away exclusively. Thinking like this shifts you away from a hands-on working model where you constantly need to replace beats. Instead, if you focus on non-exclusive leases at low prices, that same beat, over five years, could earn you a thousand dollars if marketed correctly.

This strategy isn't about quick, one-time sales; it's about long-term, sustainable income from your creations. Whether you're putting your music on beat packs, which is a feature we offer on BuyBeats.com, or marketing them individually, the idea is to maximize their earning potential over time. For instance, you could compile twenty beats into a pack and offer them for $10 or $20.

Some producers might balk at this, saying, "I'm not giving away ten of my beats for just $20." But consider this: you can go to iTunes right now and buy an entire instrumental album for $9.99. So why do some producers miss out on this leverage? Often, it's because they're too caught up in their feelings.

The current market is not the time for emotional decisions in your business strategy. If your beats can get listened to and earn even small amounts, that's infinitely better than having a thousand beats sitting on your hard drive, earning nothing. It's about playing the long game, understanding the cumulative value of your work, and leveraging your assets in the most effective way possible.

This chapter is dedicated to breaking down these concepts and helping you see the bigger picture. It's about moving beyond the immediate emotional attachment to your creations and understanding the true value and potential of your music as a business asset. By maximizing the reach and earning potential of each beat, you'll be well on your way to building a more stable and lucrative career in music production.

BUILDING A SOCIAL MEDIA ASSET

Now, let's explore other assets you possess as a music producer to fully realize their potential. Building a substantial social media following, for instance, can be an invaluable asset. Any platform where you've cultivated influence and can generate income should be considered an asset. Take ValentinBeatz as an example: he had 50,000 Instagram followers, which he had built up through various activities before he discovered Buybeats.com. He used those followers to spread his message, significantly boosting his income. His social media became an asset because it enabled him to reach out and generate income by bringing more artists and music producers into the system.

Here's how these assets work within our system: Each artist and producer that ValentinBeatz brought in became an asset for him. He introduced them once, and now their activities within the system continually generate passive and residual income for him. He moved that audience, an asset in itself, to another platform where they continued to create value for him. Similarly, Beats by Casual, Monique Winning, and DJ Luigi, along with hundreds of other producers on the BuyBeats platform, are building their assets in the same way. Asset management is a key concept that many producers overlook when I talk to them. Some return after six months, realizing the power of what they initially didn't grasp. Most traditional platforms require ongoing work, but with asset management, once you set things up, they continue to work for you.

ASSET MANAGEMENT AND PASSIVE INCOME STREAMS

Creating a sample pack, for instance, is another way to generate passive income. You put it together once, market it to your audience, and then it keeps generating money over time. This concept is no different than the powder on my barbershop table in my early days, sparking revelations about how every barber shop had that same powder. Those manufacturers understood the concept of leveraging assets. You need to grasp this too. Think about spreading your products everywhere, making money for you in various places. You're more than just a beat maker or producer; you're a businessman first, who happens to produce music.

Let me share a personal truth with you. I started making beats around 1991-92, actively selling them until 1999. However, over the past 20 years, I've made millions in the beat business without directly selling a single beat. How, you might ask? In 2007-2008, when I developed the 'SellMoreBeats.com' course and invested about 30 hours into it, I was essentially building an asset. This course, selling at $47 per copy, moved around 5,000 units. If you do the math, my total earnings of $235,000, divided by the 30 hours invested, come out to about $7,833 per hour. This success was partly because I was in my own lane with little competition at the time. YouTube had just launched in 2006, and by 2010, others started teaching similar content, making it harder to sell the course.

Seeing the changing market, I shifted my strategy. I was developing a software site, BeatWebsites.com, which offered producers a template website to upload and brand their beats. With the course sales slowing down, I bundled it as a free addition for anyone purchasing the software. I had a $99 upfront fee plus a $9.99 monthly hosting plan for a single user beat website, and a $199 upfront fee plus a $19.99 hosting plan for the enterprise package. This platform generated $700,000 over a 3–4-year period before new technologies and competition emerged. By 2016, I phased it out.

This story exemplifies how I still made an asset work, even when given away for free. It underscores a crucial lesson: markets change, and clinging to old methods can blind you to new innovations and opportunities.

LEVERAGING ASSETS IN TODAY'S MARKET

Now, let's delve into leveraging your assets in today's market. Suppose you create a beat in an hour, and it sells 50 copies at $20 each over two years - that's $1,000 from one hour of work. The real challenge is figuring out how to use your time to create even more value in the future.

Imagine compiling 20 of your beats into bundles, selling each for $10, and achieving a thousand sales. That's $10,000 earned. If each beat took an hour to produce, that's 20 hours of work. Dividing $10,000 by 20 hours, you're earning $500 per hour. Understanding these concepts and recognizing the power of pushing your assets into the market will show you how the value of an asset can vary based on market conditions and timing.

These examples highlight the exponential value of building your own assets. Unlike a regular wage, where you're only compensated for the hours worked, the time spent creating assets like courses, books, real estate investments, or software can bring in returns time and again.

In the current market, saturated as it is, finding innovative ways to leverage your assets is crucial. Every hour should be focused on creating assets that continue to generate income. Failing to do so means you're not fully utilizing your potential. The goal is to transform every hour into an opportunity for asset creation, leading to substantial collective earnings in the future.

DIVERSIFICATION AND STRATEGIC ASSET DISTRIBUTION

It's important to note that while BuyBeats.com is an excellent platform for many producers, it's not the only avenue for asset distribution. Being strategic and exploring all possible venues for your assets is key. From royalties on various platforms to leasing your beats, diversification is vital. If you had the chance to showcase your products in Walmart, Target, and on Amazon, you'd take it.

Similarly, placing your beats across diverse platforms ensures they continuously work for you.

CONCLUSION: THE INNOVATIVE NATURE OF BUYBEATS.COM

To conclude this chapter, I want to emphasize the innovative nature of BuyBeats.com. The music producers and the artists you bring to the platform are invaluable assets, continually generating revenue through their activity on the site, much like the other assets we've discussed. It's crucial to build your assets, especially as you're already networking with artists and producers. What I've done is harness the knowledge and experience I've gathered from the 1990s to the present, continuously innovating to stay ahead in the market.

One of my proudest achievements now is partnering with producers like you. By working together, we can create more income through an innovative system like BuyBeats.com. If you pay close attention, you'll notice many of the features and benefits of BuyBeats.com incorporate the lessons from this chapter. I'm leveraging all this knowledge to create a system that benefits us both. With that, we'll close this chapter and move on to our final chapter, "Mindset Mastery for Music Producers," where we'll dive into developing the mental framework essential for success in this industry.

Chapter 17

Mindset Mastery for Music Producers

Now that we're approaching the final chapters of this book, where I've shared a wealth of information with you, it's essential to delve into the heart of the matter. In this particular chapter, I'm determined to focus solely on mindset and the mental framework required to achieve your goals.

THE CHALLENGE OF MUSIC PRODUCTION

First and foremost, let me be clear – this journey isn't easy. Many aspiring producers, often swayed by marketing messages, mistakenly assume that success can be achieved effortlessly. I want to dispel that notion right away. While there are certainly strategies and tactics you can employ, you must understand that overall success demands a resilient mindset capable of surmounting all the obstacles that inevitably lie ahead.

On this path, you'll encounter countless rejections and moments of frustration. However, it's crucial to maintain the mindset that, as they say, there's light at the end of the tunnel. You must keep pushing toward that light.

DAILY REWARDS OF PERSISTENCE

The most practical revelation I can offer you is this: hard work is non-negotiable. The rewards are substantial. I experience the joy of daily rewards from the work I initiated just a few years ago. When those rewards come, it's an incredible feeling, knowing that I've achieved my goals and exceeded milestones. It's a moment to savor.

Yet, even when you reach such heights, quitting is not an option. Once you've committed your mind to a goal, there's no room for acceptance of anything else.

In this chapter, I aim to provide you with insights that have worked for me, in the hope that they may work for you too. Welcome to "Mindset Mastery for Music Producers."

When we discuss the concept of a mental framework, we're essentially delving into the unique blend of personal beliefs, attitudes, and thought patterns that shape your approach to music production and your career. Imagine a room with a hundred people; each of them will have a distinct mentality that influences how they perceive and tackle challenges. It's crucial to recognize that you possess your own mental framework, and the more you understand it, the better positioned you are to deal with various situations and enhance your chances of success.

THE ROLE OF RESILIENT MINDSET

It's essential to grasp that even if you possess exceptional technical production skills, being the best music producer alone won't guarantee success. Your mentality plays a pivotal role in propelling you toward success or keeping you stagnant for years. As I mentioned at the start of this book, it's often not the most skilled producer but the smartest one who prevails. When we speak of being "smart," we're referring to your mental framework, your mindset, and how you think.

Understanding this, it's crucial to realize that your determination, resilience, and creativity all play critical roles in your journey towards success. For me personally, challenges often fuel my creativity. When I encounter roadblocks, something within me triggers, and I become incredibly creative. I refuse to give up; my mind becomes a wellspring of ideas until I find a solution. This mindset is a part of my framework, something I do instinctively. However, some people, when faced with pressure, falter and lose belief in themselves, leading to setbacks that may take years to overcome. Guarding against such thinking is vital.

As a creative, you have a deep passion for your craft, but submitting your work for evaluation can be discouraging. You're at the mercy of others' judgments, and sometimes, that can be disheartening. However, having multiple outlets to showcase your music and various avenues for its appreciation can make a world of difference.

Let's take the example of Grammy award-winning producer Rockwilder, a close friend of mine. His determination to get his music on the radio stemmed from friends who doubted his skills. It was their skepticism that fueled his determination to prove them wrong. Sometimes, it takes a few naysayers or critics to ignite that creative spark within you, propelling you to achieve something you never thought possible. Rockwilder often shares the story of Redman's criticism of one of his beats, which ultimately led to the creation of one of Hip Hop's biggest records ever, "Da Rockwilder." This is the kind of relentless mentality you must cultivate. Be unyielding, and know that as you refine your skills and craft, you'll demonstrate your greatness to yourself and the world.

The music industry sees a constant influx of producers due to technological advancements. It's a crowded space, but you mustn't let that discourage you. You must remain open-minded, exploring multiple avenues to achieve your goals. Sometimes, it's the accumulation of small victories that eventually leads you to your desired destination.

Remember, you're not alone in facing roadblocks. Both beginners and seasoned producers experience rejection. It's a natural part of presenting your music to others who may not share your enthusiasm for it. However, rejection should never be a reason to stop pursuing your dreams.

Now, when it comes to using BuyBeats.com, maintaining a positive mindset is crucial. Approaching the platform with optimism sets you up to overcome initial challenges, including rejection. Not everyone will appreciate your work as much as you do. I've encountered producers who weren't interested in what I had to offer despite believing in the value of my vision. I've learned not to dwell on it because I know that there are producers out there making money through a system I created. I have to take the good with the bad and keep on moving with positive thoughts.

On BuyBeats.com, there are numerous producers who have found success. Take this as a conviction that you too can achieve success. While obstacles will undoubtedly arise, the fact that others have done it means you can follow the same system and achieve your goals. This is a source of motivation for me, and it should inspire you as well.

UNWAVERING DETERMINATION

Persistence has been one of my core character traits for as long as I can remember. It's challenging to tell me "no" or make me believe that "no" is the final answer. In my mental framework, "no" often means "not right now," but it doesn't equate to "impossible." It all depends on how you perceive it. Some people hear "no" and shut down, refusing to explore other options. That's not my approach. I persist in pursuing what I need, even if it means finding a different way or possibly encountering more rejection. This determination is an integral part of my mental framework.

THE POWER OF CLEAR GOALS

Having clear goals is equally crucial. Setting specific objectives gives you a target to aim for, and you'll continue to strive until you've achieved them. It's surprising how often I ask people about their goals, and they have nothing laid out. Without a roadmap or a plan, it becomes challenging to stay persistent and determined. As one of my first mentors told me, "If you don't have a plan, you plan to fail." It's a well-known saying, but it holds undeniable truth.

THE MENTORSHIP ADVANTAGE

This underscores the importance of having mentors. Mentors can help shape your mental framework. Being around successful individuals has a profound impact on your mindset. Just as negativity can be contagious, positivity and success can rub off on you. Surrounding yourself with positive influences reinforces the right mental state.

I personally gravitated toward mentors like David, Tyler G. Hicks and many other millionaires because I value the insights they share. Their teachings revolve around persistence, resilience, and imparting key nuggets that have shaped my own mental framework. Consider this: how many millionaires do you have in your phone contacts that you can call for mentally stimulating conversations? If you don't have any, it's something you should actively work on.

CONTINUOUS LEARNING FOR TRANSFORMATION

Lastly, I want to stress the importance of continuous learning. Never stop seeking new information. Sometimes, a single piece of knowledge can completely transform your perspective and lead to different achievements.

BONUS CHAPTERS AND ACTIONABLE PLANS

In the following chapters, you'll find some bonus material designed to enhance your mental framework. These chapters are meant to challenge your thinking and provide actionable plans to help you achieve your goals. You'll also discover a worksheet for the next 12 months to keep you on track for significant progress. However, it's crucial to commit to these resources.

COMMITMENT TO PROGRESS

I've encountered individuals I've shared valuable information with, only to find out months later that they hadn't taken any action – that's procrastination. Don't let procrastination hold you back; commit to your growth and progress.

Chapter 18

Sample Marketing Plan: A Blueprint Tailored for Music Producers

In this book, I've prepared a sample marketing plan to provide you with valuable insights and a structured approach to enhance your marketing efforts, much like how I progressively built up Buybeats.com. Just as I didn't tackle everything at once, but instead started with specific areas, gathered feedback, and analyzed data before optimizing, your marketing journey will involve gradual progress. It's important to understand that success doesn't happen overnight. Some individuals who quickly thrive on Buybeats.com often already have an established infrastructure. However, for those starting from scratch, achieving success is entirely feasible with the right marketing outreach plan and diligent analytics to track your progress and adapt accordingly.

The following sample marketing plan is designed to stimulate your creativity and provide a clear path to follow in your marketing endeavors. So, without further ado, let's dive into these essential points to help you navigate your marketing journey successfully.

WEEK 1: MARKET RESEARCH AND ANALYSIS

- **Day 1:** Study the music production industry trends and the role of affiliate marketing.
- **Day 2:** Research the target audience: music producers and recording artists.

- **Day 3:** Analyze competitor platforms like Beatstars.com and Airbit.com. Learn what they offer in comparison to BuyBeats.com. This helps to express the value while prospecting.
- **Day 4-7:** Identify opportunities in the affiliate program as explained in Chapter 8.

WEEK 2: TARGET AUDIENCE IDENTIFICATION

- **Day 1:** Create detailed personas of potential music producers and recording artist customers.

Sample Persona: Trap Beat Producer on Instagram
Name: Alex
Age: 28
Location: Atlanta, Georgia
Instagram Handle: @TrapMasterBeats
Bio: " 🔥 Trap Beat Producer | BeatStars Link in Bio | Ready to Elevate My Beats! 🎶 "
Followers: Less than 3,000

Description:
Alex is a 28-year-old music producer based in Atlanta, Georgia. He specializes in creating trap beats and showcases his work exclusively on Instagram. His Instagram handle, @TrapMasterBeats, reflects his passion for producing trap music. In his bio, he provides a link to his BeatStars profile, indicating that he's open to selling his beats online.

Alex is eager to improve his production skills and is open to learning from others who can provide value to his journey. He is active on Instagram but has a relatively small following of less than 3,000 followers. He's at a stage where he's looking to grow his

> online presence, connect with fellow producers, and potentially monetize his beats more effectively.
>
> Understanding personas like Alex will help you tailor your marketing efforts to reach music producers who fit this profile, offering them valuable insights and opportunities to collaborate or promote BuyBeats.com.

- **Day 2:** Understand their music genre preferences, production needs, and online behavior.
- **Day 3-7:** Segment your audience based on their music production interests and experience levels.

WEEK 3: COMPETITIVE ANALYSIS

- **Day 1-2:** Highlight key differences between BuyBeats.com and competitors.
- **Day 3-4:** Craft compelling messages focusing on BuyBeats.com's unique features.
- **Day 5-7:** Prepare responses to common objections and showcase affiliate program benefits as per Chapter 8.

WEEK 4: SETTING CLEAR MARKETING OBJECTIVES

- **Day 1:** Define specific marketing objectives aligned with affiliate goals.
- **Day 2-4:** Determine measurable KPIs such as affiliate sign-ups, beat plays, and revenue.

Key Performance Indicators (KPIs) are specific metrics that allow you to gauge how well your strategies are performing. In this context, you'll want to choose KPIs that are relevant to your role as an affiliate marketer for BuyBeats.com.

Here are the KPIs you should consider:

Affiliate Sign-Ups: This KPI measures the number of music producers and recording artists you successfully refer to become affiliates on BuyBeats.com. It's a crucial metric as it directly correlates with your potential to earn commissions from their activities.

Beat Plays: This KPI tracks the number of times beats are played on BuyBeats.com through your referral links. It's important because it can lead to stream revenue and increased earnings for you.

Revenue: Your ultimate goal is to generate income through your affiliate marketing efforts. Track the revenue you earn from various income streams, including subscription profits, stream revenue, beat sales commissions, and more.

By setting and measuring these KPIs, you'll be able to assess the effectiveness of your marketing strategies. If you find that certain tactics are driving more affiliate sign-ups or beat plays, you can allocate more resources to those strategies. Additionally, these KPIs will help you stay motivated and focused on achieving your affiliate marketing goals on BuyBeats.com.

- **Day 5-7:** Set achievable targets for customer acquisition and income generation.

WEEK 5: DEVELOPING A UNIQUE VALUE PROPOSITION

- **Day 1:** Create unique value propositions based on BuyBeats.com's affiliate program.
- **Day 2-4:** Customize value propositions for different segments (producers, artists).
- **Day 5-7:** Test and refine value propositions through feedback and A/B testing.

WEEK 6: CRAFTING MARKETING STRATEGIES AND TACTICS

- **Day 1-2:** Develop content marketing strategies, focusing on promoting beats and the affiliate program.
- **Day 3-4:** Plan social media campaigns to attract music producers and artists.
- **Day 5-6:** Create an email marketing plan targeting potential affiliates.
- **Day 7:** Share blog posts using the blue share button as explained in Chapter 11.

WEEK 7: BUDGET ALLOCATION

- **Day 1:** Allocate a budget for paid advertising campaigns targeting the music production industry.
- **Day 2-4:** Determine budget allocation for content creation and distribution.
- **Day 5-7:** Allocate resources for email marketing tools and social media ads.

WEEK 8: CONTENT CREATION AND DISTRIBUTION

- **Day 1-4:** Create high-quality content about the affiliate program and its benefits.
- **Day 5-6:** Share informative blog posts and How-To videos on BuyBeats.com.
- **Day 7:** Share content through email marketing and social media using blue share buttons.

WEEK 9: SOCIAL MEDIA MARKETING

- **Day 1-2:** Share beats, affiliate program benefits, and success stories on social media.
- **Day 3-5:** Engage with followers, answer questions, and build a community.
- **Day 6-7:** Collaborate with other producers and artists for cross-promotion.

WEEK 10: SEARCH ENGINE OPTIMIZATION (SEO)

- **Day 1-3:** Optimize blog posts and website content with relevant keywords.
- **Day 4-5:** Build backlinks from music-related websites to increase visibility.
- **Day 6-7:** Monitor SEO performance and make necessary improvements.

WEEK 11: EMAIL MARKETING

- **Day 1-3:** Send personalized emails to potential affiliates, highlighting the affiliate program.
- **Day 4-5:** Create automated email sequences to nurture leads and encourage sign-ups.
- **Day 6-7:** Analyze email campaign results and adjust strategies accordingly.

WEEK 12: ADVERTISING CAMPAIGNS

- **Day 1-2:** Launch paid advertising campaigns targeting music producers and recording artists.
- **Day 3-4:** Monitor ad performance and optimize based on conversion rates.
- **Day 5-7:** Allocate budget to the best-performing ads and channels.

WEEK 13: MEASUREMENT AND ANALYTICS

- **Day 1-3:** Track key metrics and KPIs to assess marketing effectiveness.
- **Day 4-5:** Analyze data to identify areas for improvement and optimization.
- **Day 6-7:** Generate reports to share insights with the team and make data-driven decisions.

WEEK 14: CONTINUOUS OPTIMIZATION AND ADAPTATION

- **Day 1-3:** Implement changes based on data analysis and audience feedback.
- **Day 4-5:** Experiment with new marketing strategies and tactics.
- **Day 6-7:** Continuously adapt to evolving trends and customer preferences to maximize affiliate program success.

This comprehensive marketing plan takes into account the specific information provided in the chapters and provides a step-by-step guide for music producers and recording artists to effectively promote BuyBeats.com to their target audience while leveraging the affiliate program.

Chapter 19

Artificial Intelligence: 10 AI Tools That Can Enhance Music Producers' Success

As we near the end of this book, I'd like to emphasize that much of the knowledge I've shared with you is based on my years of experience and insights into what BuyBeats.com offers its user base. But now, I want to introduce you to a game-changer: Artificial Intelligence (AI) tools that are rapidly gaining prominence in the world of marketing and content creation.

To illustrate the potential of AI, let's start with a fascinating example. The cover of this book featuring a young man in a studio with money on the counter was entirely generated by AI. I simply provided a detailed prompt, describing the scene I envisioned, including specific elements and the ambiance of a modern studio. Within seconds, AI delivered the image you see on this book's cover. The platform I used, called Night Cafe, offers a cost-effective solution for generating images. In my case, it cost me less than a penny to create this captivating cover, as I had purchased 100 credits for around $5, which allowed me to generate numerous images. The power of AI in image generation is nothing short of remarkable.

So, how does this relate to you and your journey on BuyBeats.com? Well, AI tools have evolved to the point where you no longer need to search extensively or hire expensive designers to create eye-catching visuals for your content. You can utilize AI platforms like Night Cafe and even ChatGPT's image generation capabilities. These tools allow you to input your criteria and prompts, and AI will generate images that match your descriptions. This newfound accessibility to AI-driven image generation can significantly enhance your marketing efforts, making it easier to attract your target audience, whether for blog posts, social media, or other content creation needs. Let's delve deeper into the world of AI and explore ten AI tools that can revolutionize your music production career and boost your success.

ELEVATING YOUR BEATS WITH AI MIXING AND MASTERING

As an owner of a production site, I frequently come across various music productions, especially when it comes to judging beat battles. One aspect that some producers may not be fully aware of is the availability of AI tools for mixing and mastering. These AI tools play a significant role in enhancing production quality, not only on our website for beat battles but also across the music industry. The quality of your mixes and mastering matters not just for beat battles but also for presenting your work to potential clients and customers. Therefore, it's crucial to explore the AI solutions that can help you achieve professional-grade results.

Here are some of the key benefits of using AI mixing and mastering tools in your music production journey:

Consistency: AI tools offer consistent results, ensuring that your tracks sound polished and well-balanced every time. This is particularly valuable for beat battles, where judges and listeners expect high-quality audio.

Efficiency: Traditional mixing and mastering can be time-consuming and require specialized knowledge. AI tools streamline the process, allowing you to focus more on your creative aspects while leaving the technicalities to the AI.

Accessibility: AI solutions make professional-quality mixing and mastering accessible to a broader audience, including producers who may not have extensive audio engineering expertise.

Here are a few notable AI tools that you can consider for your music production needs:

LANDR

AI Mastering: LANDR's AI mastering tool is renowned for its ability to elevate the sound quality of your tracks effortlessly.

AI Mixing: LANDR also provides AI mixing services, allowing you to fine-tune and enhance your mixes.

Aria Mastering

AI Mastering: Aria Mastering offers AI-driven mastering services with customizable settings, ensuring your tracks meet your unique preferences.

These AI tools are designed to empower producers like you to enhance the quality of your beats and music productions. Whether you're preparing for a beat battle, presenting your work to potential clients, or releasing music to a wider audience, leveraging AI mixing and mastering can be a game-changer.

EMBRACING AI FOR CREATIVE MELODIES

There was a time when I used to produce beats more frequently than I do now, and during those days, I often struggled to come up with fresh and diverse melodies. However, as I mentioned earlier in this book, with the advancements in AI and what it's capable of, I have completely embraced it as a valuable tool in music production.

Think about it this way – if you're hesitant about using AI, consider your current production methods. Do you mic up all the instruments, bringing in various musicians to play them? Or do you use sampling devices, keyboards, and other tools to trigger instrument sounds? The answer is likely the latter. You have an array of instruments and sounds at your disposal without needing to bring in live musicians. AI takes this convenience to the next level in your music production journey.

So, how can anyone judge it negatively? AI is simply another tool to enhance your music production. If you ever find yourself struggling to come up with a melody, AI can be your creative partner. You can sing or hum a melody into a microphone, and AI can help you transform it into a unique composition. With AI, you can explore new possibilities and overcome creative blocks.

Here are some AI resources that can assist you in composing melodies:

AI Music Composers

OpenAI's MuseNet: MuseNet is an AI-powered music generator that can create compositions in various styles and genres. It's designed to be user-friendly and can assist you in generating melodies, harmonies, and even complete tracks.

Google's Magenta Studio: Magenta Studio offers free AI-powered tools, including plugins like Drumify and Interpolate. These tools can help you create drum patterns and interpolate melodies, adding depth and creativity to your compositions.

By incorporating AI music composers into your creative process, you can tap into a world of possibilities, expand your musical horizons, and break through creative barriers. Embrace AI as a valuable ally in your music production journey, and you'll discover new avenues for artistic expression.

HARNESSING AI FOR EFFECTIVE MUSIC MARKETING

Marketing music in today's digital landscape demands a strategic approach that's both efficient and data-driven. This is where AI (Artificial Intelligence) comes into play. AI tools are transforming the music marketing landscape by providing musicians and music producers with powerful capabilities to enhance their promotional efforts.

AI TOOLS FOR MUSIC MARKETING:

Content Creation

Lyric and Melody Generators: AI-driven tools can help you generate lyrics and melodies quickly. This is incredibly useful for artists looking to create content at a faster pace, experiment with new ideas, or overcome writer's block.

Automated Music Video Creation: AI can analyze your music and create engaging music videos by matching visuals with the mood and tempo of your songs. This not only saves time but also adds visual appeal to your music promotion.

Social Media Management

Content Scheduling: AI-powered social media management platforms can schedule posts at optimal times, ensuring that your content reaches your target audience when they're most active.

Automated Responses: AI chatbots can engage with fans and followers in real-time, answering common questions and providing information, even when you're not online.

Predictive Analytics: AI can analyze social media data to predict trends, identify key influencers, and suggest content strategies that resonate with your audience.

Audience Analytics

Demographic Insights: AI tools can provide in-depth demographic data about your audience, helping you tailor your marketing efforts to reach specific age groups, locations, and interests.

Behavioral Analysis: AI can track user behavior, such as which songs they listen to most, where they discover your music, and what actions they take after listening. This insight helps you refine your marketing strategy.

Predictive Audience Engagement: AI algorithms can predict which audience segments are most likely to engage with your music, allowing you to focus your efforts on those who are most likely to become dedicated fans.

Streamlining Marketing Efforts with AI

Personalization: AI enables you to personalize your marketing campaigns for individual fans. You can send tailored messages, recommend songs based on their preferences, and create a deeper connection with your audience.

Efficiency: AI-driven automation streamlines routine marketing tasks, allowing you to allocate more time and resources to creative endeavors. It ensures that your marketing efforts are consistently active even when you're not actively managing them.

Data-Driven Decision-Making: AI processes vast amounts of data to provide actionable insights. This data-driven approach helps you make informed decisions, optimize your marketing budget, and focus on strategies that yield the best results.

In conclusion, AI tools are a game-changer for musicians and music producers when it comes to marketing music effectively. They offer content creation, social media management, and audience analytics solutions that save time, improve engagement, and enhance the overall impact of your music promotion efforts. Embracing AI in your music marketing strategy can set you on a path to success in the competitive music industry.

Automation is a game-changer in the world of marketing, especially for music producers. It allows you to streamline your processes, reach your audience more effectively, and ultimately save both time and money. Below, I'll introduce you to some key areas where automation can make a significant impact:

Email Marketing Automation: Tools like Mailchimp, ConvertKit, and HubSpot offer automated email marketing solutions. You can create email sequences, segment your audience, and send targeted messages, all on autopilot.

Social Media Scheduling: Platforms such as Buffer, Hootsuite, and Later allow you to schedule and automate your social media posts. Plan your content in advance and have it posted at optimal times for your audience.

Chatbots: Chatbots like MobileMonkey and ManyChat enable you to automate customer interactions on your website or social media. They can answer common questions, capture leads, and provide 24/7 support.

Content Curation: Tools like Feedly and ContentStudio can help you discover and share relevant content from various sources within your niche. Automate content curation to keep your audience engaged.

Analytics and Reporting: Platforms such as Google Analytics and Sprout Social provide automated insights and reports. Monitor the performance of your marketing efforts and adjust your strategies accordingly.

Ad Campaign Optimization: Ad platforms like Google Ads and Facebook Ads offer automated bidding and optimization features. Maximize the effectiveness of your ad campaigns without manual adjustments.

CRM Systems: Customer Relationship Management (CRM) software such as Salesforce, Zoho CRM, and HubSpot CRM automate customer data management, lead tracking, and communication.

E-commerce Automation: If you sell merchandise or music online, platforms like Shopify and WooCommerce provide automated e-commerce solutions, including order processing and inventory management.

AI-Driven Chat Support: Integrating AI-powered chat support, like Intercom, can automate customer interactions on your website, assisting with inquiries and improving user experience.

Marketing Automation Platforms: Comprehensive marketing automation tools like HubSpot, Marketo, and Pardot offer end-to-end automation for marketing campaigns, lead nurturing, and customer engagement.

By exploring these areas and leveraging the power of automation, you can focus more on your music production and creative process while your marketing efforts continue to work efficiently in the background. Remember that each of these tools and platforms offers unique features, so conducting some research and finding the ones that best suit your needs is essential.

Chapter 20

Supercharge Your Progress: Propel Goals with 8 Step Formula!

In the dynamic world of music production, achieving goals requires a unique blend of creativity, discipline, and strategic planning. Supercharging your progress involves not only setting ambitious goals but also implementing effective strategies to stay motivated and on track. This chapter will guide you through the process of setting and achieving goals as a music producer, using principles that can be applied to any creative endeavor.

STEP 1: DEFINE YOUR VISION

The first crucial step is to define your long-term vision.
Begin by taking a moment to reflect on your musical aspirations. Ask yourself questions like:

- **What kind of music do you want to create?** Are you passionate about electronic dance music, classical compositions, or hip-hop beats? Define the genre or style that resonates with you the most.
- **What impact do you want to have on your audience?** Think about the emotions, stories, or messages you want your music to convey. Consider how you want your audience to feel when they listen to your tracks.

Establishing a clear vision will serve as the guiding light for your journey.

Imagine your vision as a lighthouse in the distance, illuminating your path in the vast sea of music production. It provides you with direction and purpose. Your vision should excite and inspire you, driving your passion for music production.

Write down your ultimate goals.

These goals can be ambitious and long-term, such as:
- **Producing a full-length album** that showcases your unique style and creativity.
- **Collaborating with renowned artists** who share your musical vision and can bring new dimensions to your work.
- **Performing at major festivals** where your music can reach a broad audience and create memorable experiences.

By defining your vision and setting your goals, you are laying the foundation for your music production journey. These goals will serve as your destination points, and your vision will guide your every musical endeavor. With a clear sense of purpose and direction, you'll be better equipped to plan and achieve your goals as a music producer. Remember, your vision is the heart of your creative journey, and it's what will keep you motivated and focused as you progress in your music production career.

STEP 2: BREAK DOWN GOALS INTO MILESTONES

Once you have your long-term vision, it's time to break it down into smaller, achievable milestones.

Think of these milestones as stepping stones that bridge the gap between where you are now and your ultimate goals. Breaking your vision into smaller pieces makes the journey more manageable and less overwhelming.

Here's how to go about it:
1. **Identify Your Ultimate Goal**: Start by reiterating your long-term vision. Let's say your vision is to release a full-length album that showcases your musical prowess.
2. **Create Specific Milestones**: Break your ultimate goal into specific, measurable milestones. For example:
   - **Complete Three Songs in Three Months**: One milestone could be to compose, produce, and record three high-quality songs within the next three months. This focuses your efforts on creating content for your album.
   - **Master Production Techniques**: Another milestone might involve mastering the production techniques specific to your chosen genre. This could involve improving your mixing and mastering skills or experimenting with different instruments and sounds.
   - **Establish Music Industry Connections**: Networking is crucial in the music industry. Set a milestone to establish connections within the industry, such as reaching out to other musicians, producers, or music professionals. Attend industry events or use social media to connect with like-minded individuals.

Illustration: A timeline with milestones marked

Why Break Goals into Milestones?

Breaking down your long-term vision into milestones serves several purposes:
- **Focus**: Each milestone provides a clear focus for your efforts. It's easier to work towards a specific target rather than a vague, distant goal.

- **Motivation**: Achieving these smaller milestones provides a sense of accomplishment and motivation to keep moving forward.
- **Measurement**: Milestones are measurable, allowing you to track your progress and make necessary adjustments to your plan.
- **Manageability**: The journey becomes less overwhelming when you have a series of achievable steps.

By breaking down your ultimate goal into manageable milestones, you can methodically work towards your long-term vision while staying motivated and organized throughout your music production journey.

STEP 3: CREATE SPECIFIC MILESTONES

Once you've established your long-term vision, the next critical step is to create specific milestones that act as stepping stones toward achieving your ultimate goals. Think of these milestones as the essential checkpoints on your journey, helping you track your progress and maintain focus.

Here's how to effectively create specific milestones:

1. **Identify Your Ultimate Goal:** Begin by revisiting your long-term vision. For example, let's assume your vision is to become a renowned music producer and create chart-topping tracks.
2. **Break Down Your Vision:** Divide your overarching goal into specific, measurable milestones that will propel you forward. Here are some examples:
    - **Produce a Signature Track:** One milestone could be to produce a signature track that showcases your unique style

and creativity. This track could be a representation of your musical identity.
- **Master Technical Skills:** Another milestone might involve mastering the technical aspects of music production, such as sound design, mixing, and mastering. This could include enrolling in courses or dedicating time to practice and experimentation.
- **Build an Online Presence:** In today's digital age, establishing an online presence is crucial. Create a milestone to build a strong online presence through social media, a website, or platforms like SoundCloud or YouTube. This can help you reach a wider audience and connect with fans.
- **Collaborate with Artists:** Collaboration can open doors to new opportunities. Set a milestone to collaborate with other musicians or artists whose work aligns with your vision. This can enhance your creativity and expand your network.

Illustration: A roadmap with milestones and arrows

Why Create Specific Milestones?

Creating specific milestones serves several important purposes:
- **Clarity**: Each milestone provides clarity on what you need to achieve next, ensuring that you stay on the right path towards your ultimate goal.
- **Motivation**: Achieving these specific milestones provides a sense of accomplishment and fuels your motivation to keep pushing forward.
- **Progress Tracking**: Milestones are measurable, enabling you to track your progress effectively. You can see how far you've come and what remains to be done.

- **Manageability**: Breaking your vision into smaller, achievable steps makes the journey less overwhelming. It allows you to focus on one milestone at a time while maintaining a clear sense of direction.

By creating specific milestones tailored to your long-term vision, you can navigate your music production journey with purpose and determination. These milestones will keep you on track, motivated, and organized as you work towards your goals in the music industry.

STEP 4: DEVELOP A DETAILED PLAN

After defining specific milestones, the next vital step is to create a comprehensive plan that outlines the precise tasks and actions necessary to achieve each milestone. A detailed plan acts as your roadmap, guiding you through your music production journey and helping you overcome challenges effectively.

Here's how to go about developing a detailed plan:

1. **Connect with Your Milestones:** Begin by linking each milestone to the specific tasks required to accomplish it. Let's take the example of mastering a particular production technique as a milestone.
2. **Break Down Tasks:** For each milestone, break down the tasks into smaller, manageable steps. For mastering a production technique, this could involve:
    - **Research**: Start by researching the technique extensively. Look for resources, articles, videos, or books that can provide insights and knowledge.
    - **Online Courses**: Consider enrolling in online courses or tutorials that focus on the technique you want to master. Online platforms offer a wealth of educational content.

- **Practice Sessions**: Dedicate specific time slots for practice. Regular practice is essential to refine your skills and gain proficiency.
- **Set Deadlines**: Assign deadlines to each task to maintain a sense of urgency and discipline.

Illustration: A planner with tasks, deadlines, and milestones

Why Develop a Detailed Plan?

Creating a detailed plan serves several crucial purposes:

- **Organization**: A well-structured plan keeps you organized and ensures that you don't miss any essential steps or details along the way.
- **Efficiency**: It helps you use your time efficiently by breaking tasks into manageable portions and scheduling them effectively.
- **Resource Allocation**: You can allocate your resources, such as time, energy, and finances, more effectively when you have a clear plan.
- **Problem Solving**: When challenges arise, your plan acts as a reference point to identify potential solutions and strategies for overcoming obstacles.

By developing a detailed plan tailored to your milestones, you equip yourself with the tools needed to navigate the complexities of your music production journey. It provides clarity, direction, and a systematic approach to achieving your goals while ensuring you're well-prepared to tackle any challenges that may arise along the way.

STEP 5: LEVERAGE TRACKING TOOLS

To supercharge your progress and ensure you stay on course towards your music production goals, it's essential to make effective use of tracking tools. These tools, whether physical or digital, help you monitor your journey, measure your achievements, and maintain a positive and motivated mindset.

Here's how to effectively utilize tracking tools:

1. **Select the Right Tools**: Choose tracking tools that align with your preferences and workflow. It could be a physical planner, a digital project management app, or a combination of both. The key is to use tools that suit your style and are easy for you to access regularly.
2. **Break Down Your Plan**: Take your detailed plan from Step 4 and break it down further into daily or weekly tasks. These tasks should be manageable, actionable steps that move you closer to your milestones.
3. **Consistent Progress Tracking**: Use your chosen tracking tool to record your progress regularly. Update it with completed tasks, new insights, and any adjustments to your plan. Consistency is key to maintaining momentum.
4. **Celebrate Small Victories**: Acknowledge and celebrate your achievements, no matter how small they may seem. Each completed task is a step towards your larger goals. Celebrating these victories reinforces a positive mindset and keeps you motivated.

Illustration: A person marking off completed tasks on a calendar or digital app

Why Utilize Tracking Tools?

Leveraging tracking tools offers several benefits:

- **Accountability**: It holds you accountable for your progress. When you see tasks and milestones documented, you're more likely to stay committed to your goals.

- **Visualization**: Tracking tools provide a visual representation of your journey, making it easier to see how far you've come and what's left to accomplish.
- **Motivation**: Regularly updating your progress and celebrating achievements keeps you motivated and reminds you of your dedication to your music production goals.
- **Adjustment**: If you notice any deviations from your plan or areas where you need to adjust, tracking tools help you identify them promptly and make necessary changes.

By effectively utilizing tracking tools, you create a structured and accountable approach to your music production journey. It ensures that you stay focused, motivated, and on track to achieve your milestones and, ultimately, your long-term vision as a music producer.

STEP 6: EMBRACE FLEXIBILITY

In your music production journey, while having a detailed plan is crucial, it's equally important to embrace flexibility. The creative process is inherently unpredictable, and being open to adjustments ensures that you can adapt to unforeseen challenges and opportunities.

Here's how to effectively embrace flexibility:

1. **Recognize the Creative Process**: Understand that the creative process is dynamic and can take unexpected turns. Musical inspiration may strike at unexpected moments, leading you in new directions.
2. **Learn from Experiences**: Embrace the idea that experiences, both successes and setbacks, can be valuable teachers. If you encounter challenges or make mistakes, view them as opportunities for growth and learning.

3. **Tweak Your Plan as Needed**: Regularly review your plan and be willing to make necessary adjustments. If you discover a better way of achieving a milestone or find that your interests have evolved, adapt your plan accordingly.
4. **Stay Open to New Ideas**: Be receptive to new ideas and collaborations. The music industry is constantly evolving, and embracing new trends or partnerships can lead to fresh opportunities.

Illustration: A person navigating a winding path with flexibility and adaptability

Why Embrace Flexibility?

Embracing flexibility is essential for several reasons:

- **Adaptability**: The music industry is fluid, and being adaptable allows you to respond effectively to changes in trends, technology, and audience preferences.
- **Creativity**: Flexibility nurtures creativity by encouraging you to explore new sounds, styles, and approaches to music production.
- **Resilience**: It builds resilience, helping you bounce back from setbacks and continue pursuing your goals with determination.
- **Open-Mindedness**: Flexibility fosters an open-minded approach to music production, enabling you to experiment, innovate, and evolve as an artist.

By embracing flexibility in your music production journey, you empower yourself to navigate the unpredictable nature of the creative process and seize new opportunities as they arise. It's a key trait of successful music producers who can adapt, learn, and continue growing in their craft.

STEP 7: CULTIVATE A SUPPORTIVE ENVIRONMENT

In your music production journey, it's crucial to cultivate a supportive environment. Surrounding yourself with individuals who share your passion, understand your journey, and offer constructive support can significantly impact your motivation and progress.

Here's how to effectively cultivate a supportive environment:
1. **Identify Your Network:** Seek out fellow music producers, mentors, and friends who have a genuine interest in your musical endeavors. Look for individuals who understand the challenges and joys of your creative journey.
2. **Share Your Goals and Progress:** Openly share your music production goals and progress with your network. This transparency allows them to offer relevant advice, feedback, and encouragement.
3. **Seek Constructive Feedback:** Encourage honest and constructive feedback from your supportive network. They can provide valuable insights that help you refine your skills and grow as an artist.
4. **Offer Support in Return:** A supportive environment is a two-way street. Be willing to reciprocate by providing support, feedback, and encouragement to others in your network.

Illustration: A group of musicians sharing ideas and support

Why Cultivate a Supportive Environment?

Cultivating a supportive environment is essential for several reasons:
- **Motivation**: Your support network can offer motivation and encouragement during challenging times, helping you stay committed to your goals.

- **Learning**: Interacting with others in your field allows for knowledge exchange and learning from different perspectives and experiences.
- **Accountability**: Sharing your progress with a supportive network creates a sense of accountability, motivating you to stay on track.
- **Growth**: Constructive feedback and mentorship from your network can accelerate your growth as a music producer.

By surrounding yourself with a positive and supportive environment, you create a nurturing space where you can thrive as a music producer. Your network becomes a source of inspiration, motivation, and invaluable guidance as you progress in your creative journey.

STEP 8: REFLECT AND ADJUST

In your music production journey, regular reflection and adjustment are crucial for staying on the path to achieving your goals. It's essential to periodically assess your progress, ensuring that you're on track to meet your milestones. When necessary, don't hesitate to make adjustments to your plan.

Here's how to effectively reflect and adjust:

1. **Scheduled Reflection:** Set aside specific times in your music production journey for reflection. This can be a weekly, monthly, or quarterly practice where you assess your achievements, setbacks, and current position in relation to your milestones.
2. **Assess Progress:** During your reflection sessions, objectively assess your progress. Are you meeting your milestones as planned? Have you encountered any

unexpected challenges or successes? Take note of what's working and what needs improvement.
3. **Adapt Your Plan:** If you find that you're falling behind, facing unexpected obstacles, or discovering new opportunities, be open to adjusting your plan. Modify timelines, tasks, or goals as needed to realign with your vision.
4. **Learn from Setbacks:** View setbacks as opportunities for growth and learning. Analyze what led to the setback, identify potential solutions, and use these experiences to become a more resilient and adaptable music producer.

Illustration: A person examining a map and making adjustments

Why Reflect and Adjust?

Regular reflection and adjustment are vital for several reasons:
- **Course Correction**: It allows you to course-correct and ensure you're making progress towards your goals, even when faced with unexpected challenges.
- **Learning**: Reflecting on setbacks and adapting your plan helps you learn from your experiences and become more proficient in navigating the music industry.
- **Resilience**: The ability to adjust and learn from setbacks is a hallmark of successful goal achievement. It makes you more resilient in pursuing your music production ambitions.
- **Efficiency**: By making necessary adjustments, you can use your time and resources more efficiently, ultimately accelerating your progress.

Regularly reflecting on your journey and being willing to adjust your plan when needed ensures that you remain adaptable and focused on your long-term vision as a music producer. It's a vital practice for achieving your milestones and reaching your ultimate goals.

Chapter 21

Music Producer Self-Assessment Worksheet

INSTRUCTIONS FOR USING THE "MUSIC PRODUCER SELF-ASSESSMENT WORKSHEET"

Getting Started

Prepare Your Worksheet: Either print out the worksheet or recreate it in a digital format for ease of use. Ensure you have enough copies for regular assessments (12 copies are recommended for monthly assessments over a year).

Completing the Worksheet

Answering Questions: Start by reading each question in the 'Question Number' column. Reflect honestly on each question and write your answer in the 'Your Answer' column. Be as truthful as possible for an accurate assessment.

Scoring Your Answers: Refer to the scoring system provided with each question. Once you've selected your answer, write the corresponding points in the 'Points Scored' column.

Calculating Your Score

Tallying Points: After answering all 20 questions, sum up the points you've scored and write the total in the 'Total Score' space at the end of the worksheet.

Interpreting Your Score: Use the scoring interpretation guide provided below the 'Total Score' section to understand what your score indicates about your current standing in various aspects of music production.

Scoring

20-40 points: You may be at the early stages of your music production career or need to focus more on developing certain areas. Consider exploring new opportunities and strategies for growth.

41-70 points: You're on the right track but there's room for improvement. Focus on areas where you scored lower to enhance your career prospects.

71-100 points: You are well on your way to maximizing your potential in the music industry. Keep up the good work and continue to build on your strengths.

101-140 points: You're an established player in the industry with a strong grasp of various key aspects. Look for new challenges and ways to innovate.

141-200 points: You're at the top of your game! You've mastered the art of music production and are reaping the rewards. Consider mentoring others and expanding your influence.

Questions

1. How many assets do you have working for you?
- 1 (1 point)
- 2 (2 points)
- More than 5 (5 points)
- Less than 10 (8 points)
- 10 or more (10 points)

2. How many streams of income do you have from your music production? (BuyBeats.com system is only 1)
- 1 (1 point)
- 2 (2 points)
- 3-4 (4 points)

- 5-6 (6 points)
- 7 or more (10 points)

3. How often do you set and review personal goals for your music career?
- Rarely (1 point)
- Occasionally (3 points)
- Monthly (5 points)
- Weekly (7 points)
- Daily (10 points)

4. How do you rate your network in the music industry?
- Non-existent (1 point)
- Small and inactive (3 points)
- Growing but not engaged (5 points)
- Active and supportive (7 points)
- Extensive and influential (10 points)

5. How frequently do you collaborate with other artists or producers?
- Rarely (1 point)
- Occasionally (3 points)
- Sometimes (5 points)
- Often (7 points)
- Regularly (10 points)

6. Rate your level of comfort with marketing and promoting your work.
- Not comfortable (1 point)
- Slightly comfortable (3 points)
- Moderately comfortable (5 points)
- Very comfortable (7 points)
- Extremely comfortable (10 points)

7. How often do you explore and learn about new trends and technologies in music production?
- Rarely (1 point)
- Occasionally (3 points)

- Sometimes (5 points)
- Often (7 points)
- Regularly (10 points)

8. How do you handle setbacks or rejections in your music career?
- Poorly (1 point)
- With difficulty (3 points)
- Moderately well (5 points)
- Well (7 points)
- Excellently (10 points)

9. How diversified are your income sources outside of music production?
- Not diversified (1 point)
- Slightly diversified (3 points)
- Moderately diversified (5 points)
- Very diversified (7 points)
- Extremely diversified (10 points)

10. How much do you invest in your self-development and education related to music production?
- None (1 point)
- A little (3 points)
- A fair amount (5 points)
- A lot (7 points)
- A significant amount (10 points)

ASSET DEVELOPMENT QUESTIONS:

11. How often do you review and update your music production assets (e.g., beats, equipment)?
- Rarely (1 point)
- Yearly (3 points)
- Every six months (5 points)
- Quarterly (7 points)
- Monthly or more often (10 points)

12. Do you have a plan for growing your assets in the next year?
- No plan (1 point)
- A vague idea (3 points)
- A basic plan (5 points)
- A detailed plan (7 points)
- A detailed plan with scheduled reviews and adjustments (10 points)

13. How do you leverage your existing assets to create new opportunities?
- I don't leverage them (1 point)
- Rarely leverage them (3 points)
- Sometimes, but could do more (5 points)
- Frequently leverage them effectively (7 points)
- Consistently and innovatively leverage them (10 points)

14. How diversified are your music production assets (e.g., different genres, collaboration)?
- Not diversified (1 point)
- Slightly diversified (3 points)
- Moderately diversified (5 points)
- Very diversified (7 points)
- Extremely diversified (10 points)

15. How actively do you seek new assets or investment opportunities in music production?
- Not actively (1 point)
- Occasionally (3 points)
- Regularly, but cautiously (5 points)
- Actively and with a strategy (7 points)
- Actively, strategically, and with innovation (10 points)

16. How do you approach learning new skills in music production?
- With hesitation (1 point)
- Slowly but surely (3 points)
- Eagerly, but inconsistently (5 points)
- With consistent effort (7 points)
- As a continuous, essential process (10 points)

17. How do you rate your ability to adapt to changes in the music industry?
- Very resistant to change (1 point)
- Somewhat resistant (3 points)
- Neutral (5 points)
- Adaptable (7 points)
- Highly adaptable and proactive (10 points)

18. How often do you engage in activities that boost your creativity?
- Rarely (1 point)
- Occasionally (3 points)
- Monthly (5 points)
- Weekly (7 points)
- Daily (10 points)

19. How do you handle criticism of your music?
- Very poorly (1 point)
- Defensively (3 points)
- With some openness (5 points)
- As an opportunity to learn (7 points)
- Actively seek it out for improvement (10 points)

20. Rate your level of self-confidence in your music production skills.
- Very low (1 point)
- Somewhat low (3 points)
- Average (5 points)
- High (7 points)
- Extremely high (10 points)

EVALUATE YOUR PROGRESS AND IDENTIFY AREAS FOR GROWTH.

Question #	Your Answer	Points Scored
1		
2		
3		
4		
5		
6		
7		
8		
9		
10		
11		
12		
13		
14		
15		
16		
17		
18		
19		
20		
TOTAL		

You might be wondering why you should take this worksheet and assess your progress. The reason is simple: it allows you to reflect on a year's worth of efforts. By taking these reports once a month, if you're actively working to improve your score, you're effectively contributing to your growth and development.

In any business or professional environment, assessments are key for gaining knowledge about areas for progression. Initially, you may score low on this test—say, between 20 to 30 points. But that's okay. The goal is to complete it monthly, meticulously evaluating your responses and improvements. By the end of the year, you'll see a significant difference. For instance, consider BuyBeats.com as your sole income-generating asset. As music producer, your creations are assets. Through these monthly assessments, you might add another product, like a sample kit or a beat pack, diversifying and increasing your income streams.

These questions are crafted to guide you. By the end of the year, if taken seriously, you'll have made considerable progress.

I often analyze and review my actions to ensure I meet my targets. I wrote this book in 30 days, starting December 10, 2023, and finishing by January 11, 2024. Today, as I edited on January 15th, I realize the value of this book as an asset. Written once, it continuously contributes to the program and my personal growth. So, what assets will you work on?

Remember, the key is constant self-evaluation. Use the sheets for monthly assessments, modifying them as needed. Strive to score higher with each attempt. As we close this final chapter, I hope the insights here lead you to success and prosperity.

Allen Brown AKA Fat Fingers, signing off. Peace.

Closing Remarks

To all the dedicated music producers who've embarked on this journey with me, I want to extend my heartfelt gratitude. Your commitment to learning and growth is truly commendable, and I commend you for taking the time to explore the pages of this book. Remember that success is not a destination but a continuous journey, and you've already taken the first step towards achieving your dreams in the world of music production.

As you venture forth, armed with the knowledge and strategies shared in this book, know that every challenge you encounter is an opportunity for growth and every beat you create brings you closer to your goals. If you ever find yourself in need of guidance, support, or even just a word of encouragement, don't hesitate to reach out. Whether through DM messages or our platform's website, I'm here to assist you on your path to success.

So, with newfound knowledge, unwavering determination, and a burning passion for music production, take the next step confidently. Your journey towards residual income and creative fulfillment begins now, and I can't wait to see the incredible heights you'll achieve. Here's to your success, and may your beats resonate with the world. Phase 3 may have concluded, but your journey has just begun.

www.ingramcontent.com/pod-product-compliance
Lightning Source LLC
LaVergne TN
LVHW051549070426
835507LV00021B/2495